DO NOT REMOVE
CARDS FROM POCKET

INNOVATION
AND
COMPETITION

INNOVATION AND COMPETITION

The Global Management of Petrochemical Products

ROBERT STOBAUGH

With the assistance of
James Gagne

HARVARD BUSINESS SCHOOL PRESS
BOSTON, MASSACHUSETTS

Harvard Business School Press

92 91 90 89 88   5 4 3 2 1

Portions of chapters 2, 3, and 4 are adapted from
Robert Stobaugh, "Creating a Monopoly: Product
Innovation in Petrochemicals," in R. S. Rosenbloom, ed.,
*Research on Technological Innovation, Management and
Policy,* vol. 2, Greenwich, CT: JAI Press, Inc., © 1985,
pp. 81–112. Used with permission.

Portions of chapter 6 are adapted from Robert Stobaugh,
"Channels for Technology Transfer: The Petrochemical
Industry," in Robert Stobaugh and Louis T. Wells, Jr., eds.,
Technology Crossing Borders, Boston: Harvard Business
School Press, © 1984 by the President and Fellows of
Harvard College, pp. 157–176. Used with permission.

Library of Congress Cataloging-in-Publication Data

Stobaugh, Robert B.
  Innovation and competition.

  Includes bibliographical references and index.
  1. Petroleum chemicals industry—United States—
Management. 2. Petroleum chemicals industry—
United States—Technological innovations.
3. Petroleum chemicals industry—Management.
4. Petroleum chemicals industry—Technological
innovations. I. Gagne, James. II. Title.
HD9579.C33U576 1988   338.4'7661804'0973   87-25127
ISBN 0-87584-148-1

To

Blair, Susan, Bill, and Clay

CONTENTS

Preface

This book has involved two journeys—one long and one short. The long journey began in Baton Rouge in 1947 when I entered the petrochemical industry, as a nineteen-year-old chemical engineer with Standard Oil of New Jersey (now Exxon). In the early 1960s, as a manager at Monsanto during the day and a part-time MBA student at the University of Houston at night, I began to study in a systematic way the economics and technology of the petrochemical industry. Later, my doctoral thesis at Harvard Business School and subsequent studies of the industry provided me with articles and working papers that never quite jelled as a book. Indeed, after struggling with the material for some time, I was reminded of Charles Darwin's statement that "I begin to think that everyone who publishes a book is a fool."

This disparate collection of articles and working papers served as the starting point for the short journey, which began in 1985, when Barbara Ankeny of the Harvard Business School Press encouraged me to update the old material, add material on new subjects, and integrate it into a book. Furthermore, the Press offered to provide me with editorial assistance to ease the burden and suggested James Gagne, who had written an article based on an interview with me for *CPI Purchasing*. This opportunity was too good to refuse, so Jim and I became partners in the project.

Jim Gagne not only provided excellent editorial assistance but also helped on substantive matters involving the petrochemical industry. He took the lead in integrating and editing the material and also drafted chapter 8, "The Case of Methanol." Jim did all in such a way that it was a real pleasure to work with him.

My ideas were sharpened by presentations and discussions at meetings of the Production and Operations Management research seminar at HBS and the European Petrochemical Association. Jim Gagne benefited likewise by presentations and discussions at meetings of the Instituto de Estudios Superiores de la Empresa (IESE) in Barcelona and the American Institute of Chemical Engineers.

As I have mentioned, this book was begun with a core of working papers and articles on which I had toiled for a number of years. Chapter 7 is based on concepts in my 1968 doctoral thesis and some of the articles derived from this thesis. Ray Vernon, my long-time mentor, not only supervised the thesis but provided extremely helpful and detailed comments on the subsequent work, including earlier drafts of a number of book chapters. Anyone who has worked with Ray knows that his unselfish giving of time and his incredibly insightful comments are a model of what academic aid should be. Likewise, Max Hall, who has helped me learn to write through his editing of a number of my previous books and articles, edited earlier versions of several chapters and, as usual, was excellent in his painstaking questions and reflections.

In chapter 1, I mention that I relied on my experience in oil and petrochemicals to explain some of the managerial motivations that caused the economic and technical patterns observed. I further mention that the "nine products" studied in detail in Part I were selected because of my experience with them at Monsanto. Thus, the reader is entitled to a little more information about my industry experience. While an employee of Monsanto, from 1959 to 1965, I was engaged in process innovation, international technology transfer, and commercial chemical development. Prior to Monsanto, I worked as a chemical engineer and manager for twelve years (1947–1959) at Exxon and Caltex Oil. Subsequent to my Monsanto experience, I have been a director of Ashland Oil (1977–to date), which owns Ashland Chemical, a developer and manufacturer of some petrochemicals and a distributor of many; Chairman of the International Advisory Board of Montedison (1981–to date), during the years when this large European company was making major structural changes to its petrochemical businesses; and a consultant to a number of companies, international organizations, and governments—including being the petrochemical adviser to President Nixon's Cabinet Task Force on Oil Import Control.

I owe many thanks to that incredible institution, the Harvard Business School. My thanks start with Dean John McArthur, who has done so much to encourage research, and to Senior Associate Dean Thomas Piper, with whom I have had the pleasure of working these past four years as I chaired the HBS doctoral programs. And while I buried myself in my basement study at home to work on the book, I took solace in the fact that the doctoral programs were in the good hands of Deborah Mauger, Assistant Director, and Larry Peterson, Registration Officer.

I also appreciate the support, financial and otherwise, of the HBS Division of Research, particularly that of former director E.

Raymond Corey and the current four directors, Benson Shapiro (who watches over my research), Dwight Crane, Jay Lorsch, and Thomas McCraw, along with Kathryn May, who has administered so many of my budgets so well.

Various members of the Harvard Business School Press provided aid and encouragement in completing the current manuscript. In addition to Barbara Ankeny, there was Joanne Segal, Paula Duffy, Lisa Litant, and Maria Arteta. I appreciate the thoughtful editorial work of Natalie Greenberg and the copyediting of Elisabeth Humez. I am also grateful for the comments of the Editorial Board and several anonymous reviewers.

Especially helpful were the comments of Therese Flaherty, who also aided me with the earlier material. In addition, two other colleagues at Harvard Business School were very helpful: Pankaj Ghemawat and Louis T. Wells, Jr., a coeditor with me of *Technology Crossing Borders*. Valuable comments on the early material were received from my colleagues in the Production and Operations Management area at HBS, particularly Kim Clark, Richard Rosenbloom, and the late William Abernathy.

I owe a special debt to Richard E. Caves, who was instrumental in helping me sort out the material on innovation so that it was sufficiently orderly to appear as chapters 2, 3, and 4. Furthermore, Dick raised critical questions that exposed weak logic elsewhere in the manuscript.

Several other persons provided valuable comments on the manuscript. Sidney Robbins, a very special friend and coauthor on other books, including *Money in the Multinational Enterprise,* did an extraordinarily careful reading of the manuscript that resulted in substantial improvements to chapters 1, 9, and 10. Marvin Lieberman at the Stanford Business School provided beneficial advice, especially on chapter 5. Generous help in the form of interviews and data came from many business managers and government officials who must remain anonymous.

Friends in the consulting profession contributed data as well as comments: Christine Doey of Chemical Intelligence Services, George Hegeman of Arthur D. Little, Peter Spitz of Chem Systems, Phillip Townsend of Phillip Townsend Associates, Ronald Whitfield of DRI, and Daniel Yergin of Cambridge Energy Research Associates, my coauthor and coeditor of *Energy Future.* In fact, I have benefited many years from discussions and work on the petrochemical industry with George Hegeman and Phillip Townsend;

in addition, Phil coauthored an article with me that contained the analyses which form the basis of chapter 5.

Michele Marram went far beyond the call of duty in providing statistical data and other information from the wealth of facts and figures available in Baker Library at HBS, and she did so cheerfully and enthusiastically. She was unusually adept at finding information that did not want to be found. In addition, my appreciation goes to Judith Gurney and Jane Marsden, who filled in for Michele when she was on leave.

Harry Sachinis, while an MBA student at HBS, provided superb assistance in gathering and analyzing data. For recruiting him and students that worked on earlier phases of the research, I am indebted to my long-term colleague and friend, Joan Curhan.

Furthermore, thanks go to members of the Word Processing Center, especially Rose Giacobbe and Aimee Hamel. They were always willing and able to provide quick turnarounds of material in the unrealistically short times I requested.

Beverly Davies was an essential part of the project. She not only managed to juggle the activities involved with my other endeavors, but she located hard-to-find books, kept the various editions of the manuscript straight, and typed a number of chapters—a number of times! All this she did cheerfully with an unusual combination of efficiency and tact.

As usual, I thank my wife, Beverly, for shielding me from many of the pressures of everyday life and her encouragement on this book. Most of all, she deserves thanks for putting up with probably the town's messiest study, which has been crammed full of reference material about petrochemicals for these many years. I hope that I can keep my promise and provide her with a neat study, at least for a while!

Finally, my thanks to our four children, each born on a different continent, who never complained when they were moved around the globe in my search for knowledge and adventure. It is to them that I dedicate this book.

These acknowledgments are a scant way of showing my appreciation for the encouragement and help that I received from so many people. I hope they find merit in the book, for which, of course, I bear sole responsibility.

July 1987   Robert Stobaugh
Boston, Massachusetts

INNOVATION
AND
COMPETITION

CHAPTER I

INTRODUCTION

Capitalism is a form of economic change in which entrepeneurs, in search of monopoly profits, bring forth new innovations that destroy existing business positions. The new business positions, in turn, are destroyed by subsequent innovations—the process of "creative destruction" described by Joseph Schumpeter almost a half century ago.[1] Innovation and competition, the two major components of this process, are important to the nation and to the individual firm. A nation's economic progress depends on them and a firm's profits are spurred by innovation and limited by competition.

By their very nature, innovation and competition occur over long periods of time and involve individual products. A useful way to learn about the two activities is to study the lives of products over time—hence, the widespread interest in the concept of a product life cycle. The life of a product is marked by a series of transitions from one stage to another. To a large extent, these movements can be generalized and applied to products in many different industries.

In this book, however, I focus on one industry—petrochemicals. I go beyond the general pattern of the product life cycle and address in detail the major strategic decisions that occur in the lives of petrochemical products. These strategic decisions include product innovation, process innovation, product pricing, the sale of technology, the construction of manufacturing capacity worldwide, and the export and import of products.

THE GENERAL PATTERN OF A PRODUCT LIFE CYCLE

A major event in any product's life is when the product is initially produced for profit. To achieve this first step, a firm must close the gap between known scientific principles and the embodiment of these principles in a commercial product. So the innovating firm must be in close touch with the market in order to match a technology with the needs of customers.

Successful product innovation usually leads to rapid market growth, which, in turn, attracts potential competitors. The complexity of initial operations often creates a natural barrier to entry, and the innovator may attempt to erect additional barriers to preserve its monopoly profits. But eventually the barriers are almost always overcome and competitors appear in the market.

In some instances, a competitor is able to enter by developing a modified product. In others, it enters with the same product made by a different process. The rivalry that ensues as competition grows ordinarily results in improved products, better processes, and lower prices. And at times, firms may turn to the sale of technology as an additional source of profit.

Although an innovator of new products often focuses on its home market and initial production is frequently begun there, two factors encourage the building of production facilities in a number of countries. First, the use of the product spreads around the world, thereby stimulating firms to build plants to serve global markets. Second, as price competition increases, firms often begin to seek out low-cost areas for plant sites. The buildup of plants around the world is spurred by the innovation of modified products and new processes by firms in different countries, as well as by the transfer of technology among countries. Eventually, some industries become "global"; that is, a firm's competitive position in one country is significantly affected by its position in other countries and vice versa.[2]

Concurrent with these events, a series of related phenomena typically occurs. Initially, the rapid growth of consumption characteristic of the early years of a product's life is retarded as markets in various parts of the world become saturated with the product. Thereafter, this less attractive market picture, along with fewer opportunities remaining to be exploited in the product and process technologies, causes the rate of technological change to slow down. Finally, the product itself becomes more standardized, thereby encouraging more competition on the basis of price rather than on product differentiation. Indeed, a product often moves from the status of a specialty to that of a commodity.

The lives of products or groups of products have been studied from several perspectives. Some analysts have focused on market growth, including the modification of products to maintain high growth rates.[3] Other analysts have focused on changes in competition.[4] Still others have explored the innovation process and technological change.[5] And on the global scene, scholars have studied international trade and investment.[6]

But there has been little effort to examine all these aspects of the lives of products in one study. To fill this void, I identified systematic patterns of innovation, market growth, competition, cost, price, technology transfer, international production, and international trade in the petrochemical industry. I studied primarily individual products rather than product categories to avoid the problem of a change in mix of products over time. Moreover, the individual product approach reflects the fact that the petrochemical industry is not a monolithic whole. Rather, it is a set of many different subindustries, each involving one product and each consisting of a slightly different group of manufacturers. Thus, innovation and competition in petrochemicals mainly takes place at the product level.

WHY PETROCHEMICALS?

The constant appearance of new products and processes in the petrochemical industry has marked it as a leader in innovation. Petrochemical markets have experienced a high level of competition, as firms from several industries, including chemicals, oil, rubber, and steel, have entered the business.

Not only do petrochemicals provide a good laboratory for the study of innovation and competition, but the industry is also of major importance in the world economy and is global in scope. Worldwide output approximates $300 to $350 billion annually. The United States and Western Europe each produce about one-third of the total, with the remainder split in more or less equal shares between Japan, the Centrally Planned Economies, and the rest of the world (principally the developing countries).[7] In addition, some petrochemical manufacturers are large international firms that compete on a global basis.

Although the worldwide industry is examined in the book, the U.S. industry is given the most thorough coverage. The industry is especially important for the United States. As a leading innovator of petrochemicals and the largest market for petrochemical products, the United States is the world's biggest producer and has consistently maintained a substantial export surplus. Indeed, the United States even has a positive balance in petrochemical trade with both West Germany, itself a leading producer, and Japan, which, of course, runs an export surplus with the United States in many other industries. The United States also has been a major exporter of petrochemical technology.[8]

The book should be of special interest to those involved directly with the petrochemical industry, including business managers, government officials, and academics. But it is also intended to be useful to anyone concerned with the general subjects of innovation and competition. The roles that these factors play in the petrochemical industry have implications that go beyond the limits of the industry itself.

The study's results that involve innovation, for example, should be particularly relevant to industries with high technological opportunities (pharmaceuticals and electronics, for example). The findings involving cost, price, production, and international trade should be relevant to capital-intensive industries with production processes that have substantial economies of scale, that require a "lumpy" investment in which new facilities can be added only in large capacities, and with which firms can achieve a cost advantage by learning more about their manufacturing processes (paper and steel, for example). Appendix A presents important market, supply, and demand characteristics of the petrochemical industry that may be compared with these features in other industries in order to gauge which lessons drawn from petrochemicals might be pertinent to these other industries.

Petrochemicals are commonly defined as chemical products made from petroleum; that is, natural gas, liquids recovered from natural gas, or oil products refined from crude oil. Some chemicals produced in small quantities from coal via coke ovens are, for convenience, also classified as petrochemicals. I follow the lead of the U.S. government and consider that the petrochemical industry starts with the transformation of petroleum raw materials into primary and intermediate petrochemical "building blocks." It ends with the processing of these building blocks into final petrochemical products, such as plastics, rubbers, fibers, solvents, and bulk fertilizers. These final petrochemical products are then transformed by petrochemical-user industries into thousands of consumer products, such as toys, garden hoses, steering wheels, tires, clothes, and paints, to name just a few. Appendix B lists these stages, starting with the feedstocks and ending with the commonplace products used by consumers.

ORGANIZATION AND GOALS

The book is divided into two parts. The first, chapters 2 through 8, contains a study of individual products. The second, chapters 9 and 10, is concerned with overall industry developments.*

Part I is the analytical core of the book. It contains an examination of the fundamental forces at work in the industry and the patterns that existed prior to the 1973 oil crisis. While reference is made to published sources, I relied on my experience in oil and petrochemicals and my dialogues over a long period of time with industry executives to explain managerial motivations that caused the observed economic and technical patterns.

By and large, this is a story of markets at work, allocating scarce resources in a rational manner over many years. I used basic principles of economics and technology to analyze the lives of nine individual petrochemicals, the "nine products." From the 82 most commercially important petrochemicals (as determined by value of output), these were selected because of my experience at Mon-

---

* For readers familiar with petrochemicals, Appendix C, containing a brief history of the industry, may provide a convenient means of integrating their own recollections of prior developments with the current issues discussed in the text. For those who have little familiarity with petrochemicals, the appendix will provide a useful background to understand better those issues.

santo on the issues that arose as these products moved through their life cycle. For each of these nine products, I subsequently wrote a "Manufacturing and Marketing Guide" that appeared in *Hydrocarbon Processing*.[9] In addition to my being knowledgeable about the product, four other criteria were used:

> (1) the manufacture of the product was not tied to a natural resource that could not be easily transported; i.e., the products were "foot-loose" manufactured goods; (2) the product had characteristics that enabled it to be traded internationally; (3) there were a sufficient number of producing facilities in the world to allow statistical testing of hypotheses; (4) adequate data were available on the location and timing of world production facilities.

The nine products are acrylonitrile, cyclohexane, isoprene, synthetic methanol, orthoxylene, synthetic phenol, paraxylene, styrene monomer, and vinyl chloride monomer. They are representative of basic and intermediate petrochemicals and are used primarily in the manufacture of plastics, fibers, and rubbers. On the average, they have been produced on a commercial basis for over fifty years. Annual world production of the nine petrochemicals approximates $20 billion and world trade $3 billion.[10] Appendix D shows their principal uses and the principal raw materials from which they are made. Although these products are now commodities, at one time they were considered specialties. Therefore, the lessons drawn from them will be applicable to many products that today are considered specialties.

Innovation is the primary stimulus to the changes that occur throughout a product's life cycle—product innovation for the original building of a monopoly position and process innovation for the subsequent entries of firms that destroy the monopoly. In covering both types of innovations, chapters 2, 3, and 4 provide information about a number of important management decisions. These decisions include the type of innovation that might be an appropriate target for firms of different sizes, the types and sources of knowledge needed, the location of R&D facilities, organizational needs, and the formation and maintenance of communication links. They also cover the barriers that product innovators can use to retard the entry of process innovators.

Chapter 2 lays out the pattern of creation and destruction of monopoly profits in the petrochemical industry. Based on an analysis of the nine products, this chapter identifies three major stages: innovation of a product, the creation and maintenance of barriers to entry by the product innovator, and the loss of the product innovator's monopoly as process innovators enter the business. During the first stage, there is sometimes a hundred years or more between the invention of a product and its eventual commercialization. Then the pace of developments quickens. In spite of a number of weapons that product innovators use to keep out potential invaders, process innovators usually manage to enter the business within a few years. On the average, process innovation reaches a peak in the third decade after a product is initially commercialized. About one in every six new processes represents an improvement of sufficient magnitude to be classified as a "major" innovation. The number of major innovations peaks in the first decade of a product's life and declines during each decade thereafter.

Chapter 3, describing two in-depth case studies, highlights the substantial differences between product innovation and process innovation and reveals the deficiencies of prior models of innovation. Product and process innovation are similar in some respects; both, for example, require a reduction in market and technological uncertainties and an efficient network of communication links. A product innovator, however, faces much greater market uncertainty than a process innovator and requires a far larger number of communication links, especially outside the firm. Prior models inadequately describe what is actually involved in innovation, particularly product innovation. Among others, these inadequacies include: the description of innovation as a simple linear progression from one type of activity to another; the idea that a sharp distinction can be made between "demand-pull" and "technology-push" research; and the belief that the term "maximizing profits" sheds much light on understanding the innovation process.

Chapter 4 draws on information about the nine products, the two in-depth case studies, and findings by others to address the question: Where does innovation occur and who does it? Large-market, industrialized countries containing corporate headquarters have a decided advantage over other countries as locations for product innovation in petrochemicals. In contrast, because process innovators have far fewer contacts with the market than product innovators, large-market countries have a lesser advantage over small-market countries in process innovation than in product innovation. Although there is no generally accepted theory about the relationship between the size of a firm and its level of innovation, in petrochemicals it is the large firm that has the advantage. The general pattern is that product innovators, by and large, are the biggest chemical and oil companies, followed in size by early process innovators, late process innovators, and finally, technology purchasers. Other findings reported in this chapter contradict two widely held views on competition within industries: the belief that the degree of a firm's success depends on whether it is a leader or a follower; and the belief that product innovators, by grabbing an early lead, manage to stay ahead of subsequent entrants.

The innovation of products and processes sets the stage for a host of related economic patterns, which are described in chapters 5, 6, and 7. These three chapters discuss management decisions that must be taken as an increasing number of competitors appear, both at home and abroad. The decisions include product pricing, product differentiation, reducing costs by learning within a firm, sizing plants, using one's technology in one's own plant versus selling it to other firms, building plants abroad, and exporting and importing the product.

Chapter 5 uses data on the 82 most commercially important petrochemicals to explain why price changes occur. An early entrant into a business faces a complex problem in deciding whether to adopt a high-priced strategy in order to make substantial profits quickly, or a low-price strategy to keep out potential competitors. Regardless of which strategy is chosen by petrochemical firms, the number of competitors eventually increase and cause a gradual long-term squeeze in profits.

When a petrochemical manufacturer develops a new technology that is sufficiently good to warrant commercialization, it almost always uses the technology in one of its own manufacturing facilities. At the same time, the firm has the option of selling the technology for use by an unrelated company. Chapter 6 addresses this issue, using data on 515 of the 537 plants built worldwide that make one of the nine products. In theory an innovator can sell the technology for a price such that the competitor, because of its marginal cost, prefers the product price that maximizes profits for the innovator. In contrast, this chapter presents a number of reasons why this technology-pricing practice does not seem to occur in the petrochemical industry. The role of competition proves to be crucial in the decision to sell or not to sell technology. Other factors that affect the decision include the size of the firm owning the technology, whether the transfer is international or domestic, and characteristics of the country in which the facility is to be located.

Process innovation by firms in different countries and the sale of technology result in a gradual buildup in production facilities in many countries. The buildup in foreign markets creates an incentive for firms to export. Chapter 7 uses data on the nine products to describe patterns of international production and trade. A striking feature of the patterns is the long lags between the time a product is first produced commercially and its subsequent production in a number of countries. Although a number of factors are important in determining when a country commences production, the size of the country's domestic market is especially so. Indeed, until the time of the first oil crisis, only one of the 537 plants was built in a country without a domestic market for the product. International shipments of a product typically begin only after three or so countries produce the product. Most of the early shipments can be classified as "technology-gap" shipments because they are to countries with no production. Later, shipments to countries already producing the product become important. These shipments can be classified as "balancing" shipments since they balance supply with demand in countries that experience a shortage because plants can be added only in large steps, while consumption rises gradually. Thus, instead of trade patterns developing in a one-way direction, as predicted by the theory of comparative advantage, a country can alternate over different time periods between being an exporter and an importer of any one product.

Chapters 2 through 7 describe overall patterns in which the monopoly created by the product innovator attracts competitors, the level of competition increases over many years, and international production and international trade become commonplace. Chapter 8 focuses on one of the nine products, synthetic methanol, to illustrate these patterns.

Part II, chapters 9 and 10, describes the petrochemical industry during the years since the oil crisis of 1973. Here, in contrast to Part I, emphasis is on the industry as a whole, with the nine products used only as examples.

Chapter 9 chronicles the dozen devastating years that followed the 1973 oil crisis—years of stagnant output, a slow rate of innovation, and meager profits. In addition, a new factor increased the general gloom of the industry in industrialized countries: some small-market countries rich in oil and gas began to manufacture petrochemicals primarily for the export market.

By 1985, the industry had recovered from the depressed conditions of the early 1980s, and a certain amount of optimism had returned. Paul Oreffice, Chief Executive Officer of Dow Chemical Company, stated, "I'm convinced we have an excellent future in front of us."[11] The plunge in world oil prices in 1986 improved conditions even more. Still, as of 1987 for most products, demand and prices are not sufficiently high to justify the construction of new plants. Furthermore, unanswered is an important question: How will petrochemical production in small-market nations rich in oil and gas affect the established manufacturing areas, principally the industrialized countries? Chapter 10, in addressing the future of the industry in broad terms, discusses this question and other important issues. It speaks explicitly to likely changes in industry patterns of trade, market growth, and innovation. It also replies in broad terms to two other questions: What company strategies are likely to give the best results? What changes, if any, should be made in the government policies of the industrialized countries?

Company strategies and government policies suggested for a specific industry sometimes have relevance to other industries as well. Accordingly, my views of the measures appropriate for the future development of petrochemicals can have applications to other industries depending upon the similarity of their underlying characteristics to those of petrochemicals.

PART I

Fundamental Forces and Resulting Patterns Prior to the 1973 Oil Crisis

CHAPTER 2

PATTERNS OF PRODUCT INNOVATION AND PROCESS INNOVATION

There is often a long time lag between the discovery of a product and its initial production on a commercial basis. The firm that does this initial commercial production is called a *product innovator*. Once the product innovator has established a market, however, it is a relatively short time until another firm enters the business by developing a new process to make the product. A firm that develops a new commercial process to make an existing product is called a *process innovator*. This chapter describes the origins of the nine commercially important petrochemical products mentioned in chapter 1 and the subsequent patterns of product innovation and process innovation for these products.

PRODUCT INNOVATION

Product innovation consists of the set of activities that starts with basic knowledge and ends with a new commercial product of acceptable quality and available for sale in a quantity and at a price intended to yield profits. These profits, of course, are monopoly profits because initially the product innovator is the only producer of the product. It is the prospect of monopoly profits that encourages firms to innovate new products. As of 1982, for example, one U.S. petrochemical manufacturer had received a cumulative cash flow of $22 million from a single specialty resin, or some fifty times the company's cumulative cash outflow of $450,000 spent to develop and commercialize the product. Indeed, one new product can make an important contribution to even a giant's profits. Ciba Geigy earned more than $500 million in the United States alone from atrazine, a pesticide. Du Pont's profits from nylon have easily exceeded $1 billion and are believed to have contributed as much as half of the firm's profits during the 1950s and 1960s.[1]

Although it is clear that commercializing a new petrochemical product can be extremely lucrative, there is no study available that shows the average return on funds spent to achieve this goal. Professor Edwin Mansfield and colleagues at the University of Pennsylvania have made the most systematic study of individual projects. Their work indicated that the profits of a firm that initially commercializes a new petrochemical are, on average, good—but erratic. That study indicated that the average expected profit for the first three years of a petrochemical's commercial life was two-and-a-half times the amount spent to bring the product to the commercial stage: that is, manufacture and sell it with the intent of earning a profit. All of the profits, however, were accounted for by only one-third of the products that were commercialized. For these products, the actual and expected profits were eight times the funds spent on commercialization. The other two-thirds of the products that were commercialized showed a slight aggregate loss. That study, however, gave no indication of the amount spent to develop products that were not commercialized; therefore, the overall return on funds spent in attempts to commercialize new petrochemicals is not known from that study.[2]

Nevertheless, high risks often accompany potentially high rewards. The creation of a new product involves a journey that is long, difficult, and uncertain.

In the petrochemical industry, the commercialization of a new product is seldom derived principally from a unique knowledge of basic research. Rather, it results mostly from the large number of interrelated activities required to produce a product for a selected market. The needs of commercial firms for fundamental knowledge are so diverse and unpredictable that it is not economical for them to produce this knowledge themselves. Instead, they rely on outside sources for most of the knowledge. Hence, it is not surprising that the petrochemical industry spends less than 10 percent of its total research and development budget on basic research.[3]

True, basic research, which is the search for fundamental understanding of natural phenomena, provides the foundation of knowledge that makes possible the commercial birth of a petrochemical. But this type of research, usually done in universities and government laboratories, is undertaken regardless of its commercial value. Scientists engaged in basic research, including some in industry, generally offer their results freely to their peers. In fact, a key attribute of the published results of scientific research is that they can be understood by other scientists worldwide, for if this were not the case, they would not be accepted for publication.[4]

The histories of the nine products illustrate the point that a commercial monopoly in petrochemicals is typically not built upon control over basic research. The scientists who discovered these nine products, in the seventeenth, eighteenth, and nineteenth centuries, generally were searching for knowledge, not riches, and they readily reported their results to their peers, who were mostly in the academic world. In addition to transferring knowledge through written papers, scientists also relied on personal contact. Indeed, eight who made important discoveries about eight of the nine products had some professional relationship with at least one other among the same eight scientists. In those days it was a small world, at least in organic chemistry.[5]

The history of *styrene monomer* is illustrative. Styrene monomer was originally recovered by the distillation of a natural material called "storax," of which one source was dragon's blood, obtained from a Malayan rattan palm. The first reference to styrene monomer appeared in a chemical dictionary in 1786.[6] Subsequently, articles appeared in the 1830s in French and German, including a famous one in 1839 by E. Simon, a German apothecary, who named the product "styrol." Simon discovered that styrol polymerized to form polystyrene. Further research and publications followed in England, France, and Germany. This further work included an important 1845 paper by A. W. von Hofmann of the Royal College of Chemistry in London, which contained the first clear description of styrene, as well as papers dating from 1851 through 1869 by Marcelin Berthelot in France, which described his experiments leading to the discovery of a process by which styrene could be made from ethylbenzene, the principal raw material still used today in styrene manufacture.

It was more than a half-century later, however, before serious efforts were made to commercialize styrene monomer. Naugatuck Chemical Company tried and failed around 1925 in the United States. Badische Anilin- & Soda-Fabrik (BASF), then part of I.G. Farben, succeeded in 1931, when it began making styrene monomer for use in the manufacture of polystyrene, which it commercialized at the same time. Thus, a century and a half after the product had been discovered, a German firm brought it to the market and created a monopoly. But this monopoly was not based on exclusive knowledge of basic research. Indeed, BASF did not have a product patent.[7]

Very brief histories of the other eight products also show that commercialization was not built upon control over basic research.[8]

Friedlieb Ferdinand Runge, a German chemist, discovered *phenol* in 1834. It was seventy-three years later—in 1907—when the German firm Bayer began the commercial production of synthetic phenol.

In 1835, Henri-Victor Regnault, a French chemist, first prepared and described *vinyl chloride monomer*. It was not until 1912, however, that the German firm Chemische Fabrik Griesheim-Electron obtained a patent for the manufacture of vinyl chloride monomer, establishing an effective industrial process. Finally, in 1927, Dynamit-Nobel (then part of I.G. Farben) first produced vinyl chloride monomer commercially in Germany, followed shortly by Union Carbide in the United States.

Acrylonitrile, first prepared by the French chemist Charles Moreau, in 1850, was not made commercially until 1933, again by I. G. Farben's BASF, as a raw material for oil-resistant synthetic rubber. The rubber was subsequently used by the Germans, as well as the Americans, in self-sealing gasoline tanks in airplanes during World War II, for it would seal a half-inch bullet hole almost immediately.

A. Cahours, a French chemist, first discovered xylenes in 1850 in a wood-tar distillate. Almost a hundred years later, Standard

Oil of California (now Chevron) began the commercial separation of *orthoxylene* and *paraxylene* from xylene mixtures, which had begun to be produced from petroleum just a few years before.

Charles Williams, a chemist working in Glasgow and London, first isolated *isoprene* from the pyrolysis products of natural rubber in 1860, and V. I. Ipatieff, a Russian chemist, first synthesized it in 1897. It was forty-seven years later before Standard Oil of New Jersey (now Exxon) first produced isoprene commercially as part of its program to develop synthetic rubber for use during World War II.

Cyclohexane was first synthesized in 1893 by Adolf von Baeyer, a German Nobel Prize recipient, who, though credited with being one of the founders of the German synthetic dye industry, reportedly made no profit from his research. Cyclohexane was first produced commercially by Du Pont in the United States in 1942 in its development of processes to make nylon.

As for *methanol,* there was a long time lag between the initial discovery in the seventeenth century and its subsequent commercialization (see chapter 8).

Thus, as the history of these nine products demonstrates, the commercial development of petrochemicals typically occurred many years after the initial discovery of the product. And the monopolies of the product innovators were based on their ability to build upon basic knowledge in developing the markets and the production processes by which the products could be made at satisfactory costs—the process of product innovation, which will be discussed in chapter 3. It is true, however, that some products—such as certain special types of polystyrene, or polymers containing both acrylonitrile and styrene—that encompass variations in the basic products have been commercialized in fewer years after their discovery than the long time periods mentioned above, but the commercialization still rested heavily on the process of product innovation.

A monopoly can generate high profits, and high profits attract competitors. A product innovator, however, has several weapons to repel would-be invaders of its markets.

Patents are one such weapon. A patent on the product sometimes provides the product innovator with a monopoly for years.

But in other instances, particularly basic petrochemicals and some intermediate petrochemicals, patent protection on the product is not available to the product innovator. In some cases, the steps involved in moving from the discovery of a petrochemical to its commercialization are so time-consuming that the product patent either expires by the time the product is commercialized or expires shortly thereafter. In other instances (the case for all nine products), a scientist engaged in basic research discovered the product so many years before commercialization took place that a patent, if one had existed, would have expired years before product commercialization.

Regardless of the status of the product patent, a product innovator typically has a patent that protects its manufacturing process. Thus, prior to the expiration of the process patent, any would-be competitor faces the task of developing a new manufacturing process.

In addition to product and process patents, a product innovator has four other weapons available to help defend its monopoly of the product.

One weapon is the modification of the product to make it available for more uses. In most basic and intermediate petrochemicals, which are usually liquids or gases, the scope for product modification is quite limited because the product has a set chemical formula and the major potential for improvement is in removing impurities. But in the case of polymers, elastomers, and fibers, the development of an extensive array of new or modified products with the same chemical composition is possible. Not only does the creation of new or modified products help keep competitors at bay, it also causes growth in the overall product line. For example, Du Pont created a number of different types of nylon-66—a product made from cyclohexane—thereby dramatically expanding its use.

"Learning" about the process is the second weapon that the product innovator can use. This learning enables the company's technical staff and operators to remove bottlenecks in the existing plant so as to provide the additional capacity needed as the market for the product grows. Such capacity can be very inexpensive, involving little capital and few or no extra employees. As an illustration of the low cost that can be involved in debottlenecking an existing plant, replacing a single pump that might cost less than 1 percent of the plant's total costs could add 10 percent to plant capacity. A series of debottlenecking projects sometimes allows the output of a plant to be doubled, but sooner or later the increasing costs of further expansion cause the economic limit to be reached, and a new plant is needed. Thus, debottlenecking helps a product innovator achieve lower costs, but only up to a point.

But regardless of whether a limit is reached in debottlenecking, learning also enables the technical staff and operators to improve the efficiency of the operations. Of course, learning could involve the product innovator's improving operations by developing and commercializing a completely new process to manufacture the product, but this occurred only once among the nine products, when Bayer, the original commercializer of synthetic phenol in 1907, commercialized a different process in 1940 (thereby becoming a process innovator as well as a product innovator).

A third weapon is to provide additional capacity by building a new and larger plant. Doing this will result in lower costs because of the economies of scale realizable in petrochemical plants.[9]

The fourth weapon is to integrate vertically toward the market so as to limit the open market available to any would-be entrant. For example, all of the early styrene monomer manufacturers also made polystyrene, so the opportunity for a new entrant into the styrene monomer business was limited by either the willingness of existing monomer manufacturers to purchase from a rival or the development of a polymer business by a firm other than one of the monomer manufacturers. And the captive market for monomer ensured by vertical integration into polymer reduced the market risk of a monomer producer's adding additional monomer capacity. But this weapon was not sufficiently effective to keep out competitors, and whatever effectiveness did exist dropped as a large open market developed for styrene monomer.[10] In any case, vertical integration is certainly not effective against a competitor who has developed a substantially lower-cost process. BASF, for example, the product innovator of acrylonitrile, was vertically integrated toward the market, but it eventually exited from the business as lower-cost producers entered.

PROCESS INNOVATION

Firms that smell the aroma of another firm's monopoly are not
easily shaken off, so the product innovator, in spite of its lead over
other firms, is unlikely to maintain a monopoly for long. Competitors inevitably appear. Thus, the net effect of all of the repellents
mentioned above is to buy the product innovator a temporary lead
over other firms. For the nine products, the average time for a
second firm to produce the same product without purchasing the
technology from the product innovator was 5.7 years, with a median of four years (see Table 2-1). These are relatively short periods compared with over fifty years' average time, so far, that the
nine products have been produced commercially. Further, there
was little difference in the lag between the initial commercialization and the entrance of the second firm among two groups of
products—those innovated in Germany, all before World War II,
and those innovated in the United States, all after the start of
World II.[11]

The size of the rewards garnered by the process innovator, of
course, is heavily dependent on the extent to which the new process is superior to existing processes. The biggest reward occurs
when the new process is so good that it makes sense for its innovator—or any firm purchasing the know-how from the innovator—
to price the product so low from a new plant that the process is
used not only in all new plants, but also causes existing plants to
be shut down. The lower production cost involved in using the
new technology also results in lower product prices and increased
market growth. For example, in 1960, Standard Oil (then called
Standard Oil of Ohio, or Sohio) introduced a new process to
manufacture acrylonitrile (by then used principally as an intermediate for making acrylic fibers). Simultaneously, Sohio cut the
price from 26 cents to 18 cents per pound, thereby causing widespread shutdowns of existing acrylonitrile plants. As is often the
case in the petrochemical industry, the specialized nature of the
old plants made it uneconomical to convert them to utilize the new
process, so they were closed and dismantled. Furthermore, virtually all companies that subsequently built plants purchased their
know-how from Sohio. Sohio's profits from this process innova-

Table 2-1
Time Lags Between Product Innovation and Initial Production by
Process Innovator, Nine Products

Product	Year of Product Innovation		Time Lags (years)
Innovated in Germany			
Synthetic phenol	1907		7
Synthetic methanol	1923		3
Vinyl chloride monomer	1927		2
Styrene monomer	1931		4
Acrylonitrile	1933		7
		Average	4.6
		Median	4
Innovated in United States			
Cyclohexane	1942		5
Isoprene	1944		16
Orthoxylene	1945		3
Paraxylene	1949		4
		Average	7.0
		Median	4.5
All Nine Products			
		Average	5.7
		Median	4

Sources: Industrial trade journals and author's questionnaire.

tion are not public information, but executives in the industry believe they have exceeded $700 million.

New processes do not always cause existing plants to shut down. In some cases they are no more efficient, or indeed are even less efficient, than existing processes. But some firms use these new processes to enter the business and share in the monopoly or oligopoly profits that exist because of the small number of participants in the business. For example, the plant of Foster Grant, when it entered the styrene monomer business in the United States in 1954, was not as efficient as plants already in use by some of the existing participants (Dow and Monsanto, for example), but the relatively high level of oligopoly profits made it attractive for Foster Grant to enter the business.[12] Even in cases in which a new process is inherently more efficient than an old one, many existing plants utilizing the old process continue to operate for many years. The capital-intensive nature of petrochemical manufacturing makes the marginal costs of operating many of the existing plants lower than the average costs involved in building and operating a new plant with the better process. And, in some instances, the new process represents such a minor improvement over existing ones that few new plants (perhaps only one) are built to use the new process. Thus, at any one time it is possible for a number of different processes to be used concurrently by different firms making an identical product.

True, in many cases the would-be process innovator fails to develop technology that is worth commercializing. In these situations, any payoff must come from patent positions and expertise that might be of use in other applications.

Categories of New Processes

The number of ways to make any given petrochemical, although finite, can be quite large. In total, during the life of the nine products through 1974, 180 new processes were developed in addition to the original processes—an average of 20 new processes per product, or an average of one every two years for each product.

For analytic purposes, new processes can be classified into two categories: *major* innovations and *minor* innovations. Major innovations are fundamentally different from existing processes, involving different raw materials or radically different reaction conditions, such as the use of vapor-phase rather than liquid-phase reactions.[13] Major innovations are especially important because they are more likely to make existing processes obsolete than are minor innovations. Major innovations represented only 29 of the 180 new processes developed to manufacture the nine products, an average of slightly more than three per product, or one every thirteen years for each.

The number and types of new processes developed for any single petrochemical undoubtedly depend upon a number of forces. For instance, the relative economic positions of different processes can be affected by relative values of different raw materials and co-products, energy costs, the cost of capital, or the development of some new technology, such as new catalysts, that could favor one process over another.

Phenol is an example of a product manufactured commercially by a number of radically different processes at the same time—four in the mid-1960s in the United States. Although all the processes used benzene as an important raw material, each used different raw materials to react with the benzene and each generated different co-products or by-products. One process, employing sulfuric acid, generated sodium sulfite and sodium sulfate, which because of their low values could not be transported over long distances for sale. Another process used chlorine, which requires large quantities of electricity and yields caustic soda as a co-product. Still another process used hydrogen chloride and generated very little co-product, but required a facility that was very costly to build. The fourth process used propylene as the other major raw material and generated acetone as a co-product. Thus, the relative economics of the different processes depended on the relative prices of propylene, acetone, sulfuric acid, sodium sulfite, sodium sulfate, caustic soda, hydrogen chloride, electricity, and capital.[14]

A key factor determining the number and types of processes developed for any product is the amount of capital that companies devote to the search. Although some companies can calculate how much money has been spent during recent years to develop new processes for individual products, few have sufficient information available for all the years—sometimes fifty or more—in which they have conducted such studies. For instance, in every year since its introduction of styrene monomer in 1931, BASF has probably spent some funds in improving its styrene monomer process. During much of this time, other companies—some of which have never produced styrene monomer—have spent money in attempts to develop new manufacturing processes. Therefore, hard analysis of the factors that determine the level of expenditure on developing new processes for individual products is out of reach. Moreover, available studies do not indicate the aggregate expenditures and returns for developing new petrochemical processes.[15]

Presumably the expenditure level for developing new processes would be decided by using a cost/benefit analysis made by companies performing the research.

One would expect a priori that the cost/benefit analysis would reflect changes occurring over time in the following four forces: first, the cost of developing a new process; second, the level of monopoly (or oligopoly) profits in the market for the product; third, the level of monopoly (or oligopoly) profits in the market for the process; and fourth, the volume of products likely to be made using the new process.

On point number one, the costs of developing a new process are likely to increase over time as the new processes most easy to develop are innovated first. In other words, one would expect processes to be developed in order of increasing difficulty. True, it is possible that such increasing costs could be more than offset by the use of new knowledge, tools, and techniques available only with the passing of years.

On the second point, monopoly (or oligopoly) profits in the product market are likely to be higher during the early years of a product's commercial life, when there are relatively few makers of the product, than later, when there are more makers. Thus, the perceived benefit to be derived from a new process would decline over time.

Third, similarly, the monopoly (or oligopoly) profits attributed to ownership of the process would be expected to decline over time as more processes became available.

Fourth, the size of the potential market for a new process expands as long as the annual production of a product continues to grow (as has occurred for the nine products except during some recession years). Therefore, the potential benefits to be derived from a new process by its innovator would be expected to increase over time, for if a new process is efficient enough, it might make existing facilities uneconomical. In practice, however, it may be that the increasing difficulty over time of commercializing a technology that is a major innovation reduces the chances that existing facilities would be rendered obsolete by any new process. But even if existing facilities were not rendered obsolete and a new process was used only for new plants, a modest percentage increase in output over a large base of production could generate sufficient needs for new capacity so that an attractive and perhaps increasing incentive to develop a new process would exist.

Thus, some forces would tend to cause an increase over time in the level of expenditure that companies would make to develop new processes for manufacturing any given product, whereas other forces would tend to cause a decrease. But the exact pattern is not predictable a priori.[16]

In the case of the nine products, from the year of the commercial birth of each product through 1974, the number of new processes developed each decade rose and then fell (see Figure 2-1). The actual number of new processes averaged three per product in the first decade of a product's commercial life, rose to four in the second decade, then peaked at seven during the third decade, and subsequently fell.[17] On the other hand, the number of *major* process innovations was highest during the first decade and gradually declined as more new processes were commercialized. Similarly, major innovations as a percentage of total innovations declined with each passing decade, from 67 percent in the first decade to 8 percent in the fifth decade. Thus, with more and more discoveries of new processes, there was a decline, as shown in Figure 2-2, in the probability that the next innovation would be a major one.[18] To be sure, even though they are unusual, major innovations do occur for old petrochemicals. For example, the process widely used today to make synthetic phenol was introduced some fifty years after that product's commercial introduction in 1907 and after fourteen previous processes had been used commercially to manufacture it. And in 1972, some forty years after BASF commercialized styrene monomer, Halcon International, an engineering company, along with two partners, commercialized a different styrene process, which produced propylene oxide as a co-product along with styrene monomer.[19]

These systematic patterns of innovation suggest that any new process that is only a minor innovation may soon face additional competition from other processes developed subsequently. In contrast, a major innovation is much less likely to face competition

Figure 2-1

Number of New Processes Developed in Each Decade of Product's Life, Average for Nine Products, Year of Commercial Introduction through 1974

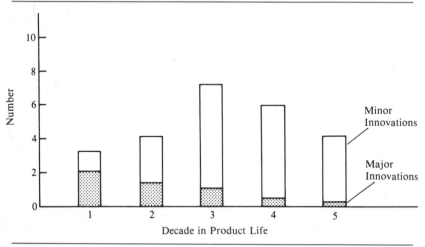

Note: Not all nine products were as old as 50 years in the period covered by this exhibit. The average number of the nine products that existed in each decade was as follows: 9 in first and second; 8.5 in third; 5.2 in fourth; and 3.2 in fifth.

Sources: Industry trade journals and author's questionnaire.

from a subsequent major innovation. The patterns also suggest that eventually the limits of technology are approached and further R&D spending on process development may yield meager results.

These conclusions are of obvious concern to managers. In addition, they shed light on the important question of why there is uneven allocation of R&D spending among industries. Richard Nelson and Sidney Winter, two Yale economists, offer two different, but not mutually exclusive, explanations.

One is that innate differences in opportunities for efficient advancement in different kinds of technology affect the levels of R&D in different industries.[20] This explanation is consistent with the above patterns for petrochemicals, since different opportunities for successful process innovations occur at different times over the life of the product, and with each passing innovation the chances of a major innovation decline.[21]

Their second explanation is that R&D activity differs because

Figure 2-2
Probability of Next New Process Representing a Major Innovation,
Nine Products, from Year of Commercial Introduction through 1974

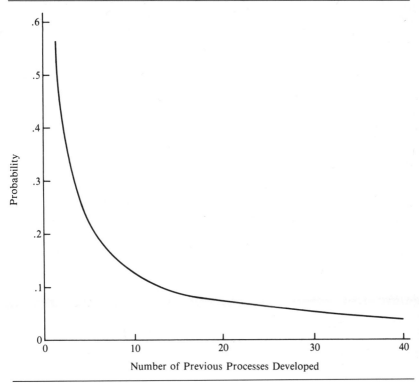

Source: Note 18, this chapter.

industries differ significantly along two dimensions: the extent to which the sponsoring firms in one industry are able to capture the benefits of their R&D, compared with sponsoring firms in another industry; and the speed and reliability of the mechanisms by which new technology is screened and used (in one industry compared with another industry). The results in petrochemicals do not support this explanation because these external forces are more or less similar for all nine products.

The view described in this chapter has been from outside the firm. It is time now to lift the veil surrounding the firm and see what goes on within.

CHAPTER 3

HOW PETROCHEMICAL INNOVATION IS CONDUCTED: TWO CASE STUDIES

How petrochemical innovation is conducted affects where innovation occurs and who does it. In order to illuminate what is involved in petrochemical innovation and the differences between product innovation and process innovation in petrochemicals this chapter examines in some depth two case studies—one involving product innovation and the other process innovation. The two cases involve activities that are typical of petrochemical product and process innovation.[1] They suggest that specific modifications in prior models developed to describe innovative activity are necessary. In addition, the findings suggest that the differences between product innovation and process innovation have important implications—both for managers in industry and for scholars concerned with the theory of innovation.

PRODUCT INNOVATION: ALPHA'S JOURNEY

Records for a nine-year period of an attempted development of a new petrochemical by a U.S. company engaged in petrochemical R&D and manufacture show the richness of real life not captured by aggregate data. The company's disguised name is Alpha. An analysis of this project highlights the importance of two key factors in the innovation process: (1) the reduction of uncertainty and (2) the communication links.

Alpha's initial goal was a halide-based polymer for use in baked-on coatings. During the nine years, Alpha's activities were confined to applied research and the preparation of basic specifications. The firm obtained its product from three different facilities: a very small one in its laboratory, which produced only ounces, designated "laboratory scale" by the company; a larger laboratory unit, which produced a total of 15 pounds, referred to as "bench scale"; and an outside custom manufacturer, who produced 500 pounds in total.

At the end of the ninth year, Alpha was deciding whether to build a pilot plant with a capacity of one million pounds a year, a step that would be necessary in order to proceed toward commercialization. If the pilot plant were built and operated, three stages in the innovation process would remain: design and construction of manufacturing facilities, start-up of these facilities, and start-up of commercial marketing activities. The alternative to building the pilot plant was to stop the project and attempt to sell to another company whatever knowledge had been acquired during the project.

By the end of year nine, Alpha had spent some $2 million on the project, three-fourths of which represented expenditures within the firm, principally salaries and related expenses. The remaining costs had been incurred primarily for services. The yearly rate of spending had risen from $100,000 at the beginning of the project to $400,000. The cost of the pilot plant would exceed $1 million, and operating costs would be at least that much again. The cost of a commercial plant would be about $12 million, and the total cost of the product innovation perhaps $20 million.

This $20 million would be substantially more costly than the $450,000 mentioned in chapter 2, which was spent in innovating a specialty resin. On the other hand, many product-innovation projects are much more costly than Alpha's. For example, in an attempt to develop a new polymer, in 1983 one firm had spent $3 million over a six-year period, reaching an annual spending rate of $1.2 million. This company was hoping to commercialize the product in 1988, by which time some $20 million would have been spent on research and development. A total of $70 million was projected to be invested through 1990, but by then profits were expected to be substantial.[2]

The project at Alpha had started when a senior research scientist concluded from a survey of literature that a certain halide-based polymer had commercial potential for use in baked-on coatings. He speculated that such coatings could be used as fire-retardant wall covering. A consultation among several members of the research department was followed quickly by a consultation between the research department and the commercial development department. (Like many petrochemical firms, Alpha had a separate department to manage the commercial development of new products.) This department was responsible for integrating the activities of specialists involved in product innovation, including the integration of the long-term focus of research with the short-term focus of marketing.[3] Figure 3-1 shows those persons and units of Alpha involved in the commercialization of petrochemicals.

Since the research department and the commercial development department favored the project, the general manager of the petrochemical division gave approval to proceeding with an evaluation. The ultimate hope, albeit quite hazy, was to commercialize a petrochemical product that could be used to make building materials that would have better fire-retardant characteristics than existing materials. The basic technology was to involve the reaction of halides and hydrocarbons, most likely through a number of steps involving reactions and attendant separations.

Reduction of Uncertainty

In this context, "uncertainty" means that the decision maker holds only vague opinions about possible outcomes and about the probability of occurrence of each possible outcome (called "diffuse prior distributions" by Bayesian statisticians). These opinions are vague because a decision in question is sufficiently unusual that there have been either no others, or not a sufficient number, for the decision maker to have formed a strong opinion about possible outcomes and the probability of different outcomes. This meaning of uncertainty is consistent with that used by other researchers in the field of innovation. But uncertainty can also have another meaning: the outcome of any single event can be uncertain although the decision maker knows all alternative outcomes and the

Figure 3-1
Organizational Units Involved in Commercialization of Petrochemicals,
Alpha Company

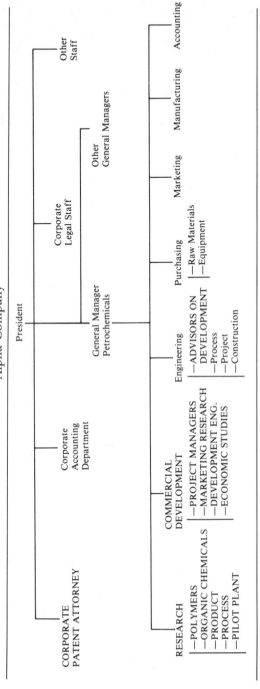

Note: Capital letters mean that a unit's, department's, or person's principal activity is innovation, either product or process.
Source: Robert Stobaugh, "Creating a Monopoly: Product Innovation in Petrochemicals," in R. S. Rosenbloom, ed., *Research on Technological Innovation, Management and Policy* (Greenwich, CT: JAI Press, Inc., 1985), p. 90.

probability of occurrence of each (in the language of the statistician, this is an uncertain drawing from a known distribution). This second instance seldom exists in product or process innovation in petrochemicals (although it does exist in many situations that are insurable and that are referred to as "risky," such as the possibility of a house fire).[4]

As Alpha's project made its way through the thickets of uncertainty, almost all starting expectations, as well as many of those adopted along the way, underwent major changes. The underlying causes of this uncertainty can be classified into two categories: market and technology.[5] These two uncertainties, in turn, resulted in open questions about price, volume, and timing. Indeed, a range of raw materials was considered in studying how to make a range of possible compounds for a range of possible uses. Throughout the twists and turns of the project, the primary technical goals remained the same: to develop a product that would deliver superior performance in a given application and to develop an efficient process to make the product.

The following examples illustrate the high degree of uncertainty encountered by Alpha at various times during its journey.

Market: Initial target was baked-on coatings, but by end of year 9, non-baked coatings, hard elastomers, soft elastomers, rigid foams, flexible foams, and adhesives had been considered. Four different types of polymers had been evaluated by the end of year 9.

Technical: Twenty different processes had been evaluated involving dozens of different raw materials and 9 different intermediate monomers from which polymers are made.

Price: Estimates of possible selling prices ranged from 31 cents to $1.11 a pound.

Volume: Plant capacities that were considered ranged from 500,000 to 50 million pounds annually.

Timing: In year 3, a critical-path schedule was issued showing that a decision on commercialization could be made in March of year 4. But by the end of year 9, a commercialization decision appeared to be some years away.

As a result of changes in the project, ten separate approvals by the general manager of the petrochemicals division were required.

Communication Links

There were communication links at Alpha both within the firm and with outside entities, especially potential customers. At the center of the links was a commercial development project manager, who was responsible for the project. This manager had no direct authority over those in other Alpha departments and so had to rely on persuasion rather than commands. His lack of authority probably increased the number of links within the company, since he did not have the luxury of setting up a direct chain of command through which his orders would flow. At any rate, he became the central figure in a complex communication network within the firm, as shown in Figure 3-2. In addition to the eight continual and five sporadic communication paths used by the project manager, there were a number of other communication links within the firm that did not flow through the project manager.

The parts of the communication network used during a given time period depended on the status of the project. Initially, the principal actors were the project manager and marketing research manager of the commercial development department; group leader, senior scientists, and analytical laboratory personnel of the research department; and the accountants who provided a record of expenditures. From time to time—at least quarterly and often monthly—reports were given to, and discussed with, the general manager.

As the project progressed, other groups entered the picture, sometimes on a continuing and sometimes on a sporadic basis. By the end of year nine, all the paths shown in Figure 3-2 had been used, many of them during the entire period. If the project were to proceed after year nine, additional communication paths would have to be created as the project moved through subsequent stages. For example, the decision to proceed with a pilot plant would create a number of paths to and from the pilot-plant section of the research department.

Very early in the project, Alpha began to create a communication network outside the firm. During the first year, the project manager made contact with an outside company—a combination

Figure 3-2

Principal Communication Paths within Alpha Company during Years
1 to 9 of Innovation of Petrochemical

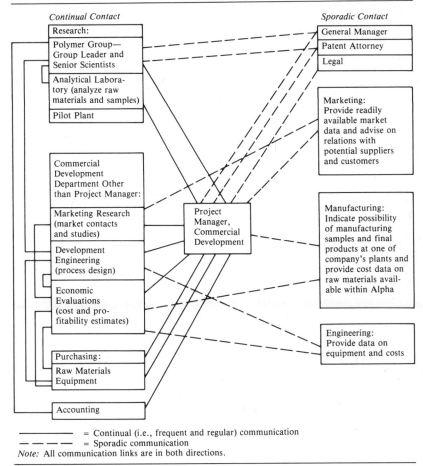

Continual Contact

Research:

Polymer Group—
Group Leader and
Senior Scientists

Analytical Labora-
tory (analyze raw
materials and samples)

Pilot Plant

Commercial
Development
Department Other
than Project Manager:

Marketing Research
(market contacts
and studies)

Development
Engineering
(process design)

Economic
Evaluations
(cost and pro-
fitability estimates)

Purchasing:

Raw Materials
Equipment

Accounting

Project
Manager,
Commercial
Development

Sporadic Contact

General Manager

Patent Attorney

Legal

Marketing:
Provide readily
available market
data and advise on
relations with
potential suppliers
and customers

Manufacturing:
Indicate possibility
of manufacturing
samples and final
products at one of
company's plants and
provide cost data on
raw materials avail-
able within Alpha

Engineering:
Provide data on
equipment and costs

————— = Continual (i.e., frequent and regular) communication
– – – – = Sporadic communication
Note: All communication links are in both directions.

Source: Robert Stobaugh, "Creating a Monopoly: Product Innovation in Petrochemicals,"
in R. S. Rosenbloom, ed., *Research on Technological Innovation, Management and Policy*
(Greenwich, CT: JAI Press, Inc., 1985), p. 93.

testing laboratory and consulting firm—that evaluated the products and advised Alpha of the probable reactions of customers.
During year two, the project manager began to contact potential
customers. By the end of year nine, Alpha had established innu-
merable contacts with outside firms.

Table 3-1 lists the principal contacts that Alpha's commercial development department had with outside firms. Undoubtedly others would be established if the project proceeded into year ten, and meanwhile, other departments had numerous external contacts. Altogether, the commercial development department contacted more than 150 different organizations, most of them numerous times. Virtually all contacts with potential customers, competitors, and consultants were intended to reduce market uncertainty. Contacts with custom manufacturers, testing laboratories, engineering firms, and raw material suppliers were intended to reduce technical uncertainty as well as market uncertainty.

In the chemical industry, manufacturers typically send, for the asking, samples of proposed new products to any firms believed capable of developing commercial uses for them, so Alpha obtained samples of potentially competitive materials from three manufacturers. These three firms and other manufacturers of potentially competitive materials gave speeches at industry meetings, at which Alpha attempted to gain as much information as possible through judicious questioning. In order to facilitate these contacts and keep abreast of raw-material prices and industry developments, Alpha's commercial development personnel attended a yearly average of twelve professional meetings dealing with market research and commercial development.

A perennial problem faced by Alpha was how to keep communication links alive over many years, given that individuals often change jobs. Alpha used frequent face-to-face contacts as well as some written procedures to help keep internal links alive. Keeping up external links posed a greater difficulty: the commercial development manager had to maintain close and frequent contacts with the outside world to ensure that proper introductions were made when a newcomer replaced someone on the communication grid.

In addition to illustrating the great amount of uncertainty involved in product innovation, the Alpha case illustrates the difficulty of developing a unique technology and matching it to the needs of a market. This case also shows that this matching requires the integration of many different specialists—scientists, engineers, operators, market researchers, and others. The integration process creates a need for frequent, effective, and swift communication among the specialists.[6]

Table 3-1

Contacts outside Alpha by Alpha's Commerical Development Department

	Individual Organizations Contacted		
Type of Organization	Number	When	Purpose
Potential customers	59	years 2–9	Determine interest in potential products
Competitors	more than 50	years 1–9	Obtain information about potentially competitive products, including samples
Consultants	9	years 1–9	Obtain specialized services, principally market reports and economic evaluations
Custom manufacturers	2	year 7	Have a 500-pound sample of a potential product made
Testing laboratories	4	years 3–9	Obtain tests of potential products
Engineering firms	1	years 3–9	Obtain estimates of plant costs
Others, including raw material suppliers	more than 25	years 1–9	Keep abreast of raw-material prices and industry developments
Total organizations	more than 150		

Source: Robert Stobaugh, "Creating a Monopoly: Product Innovation in Petrochemicals," in R. S. Rosenbloom, ed., *Research on Technological Innovation, Management and Policy* (Greenwich, CT: JAI Press, Inc., 1985), p. 94.

PROCESS INNOVATION: BETA'S JOURNEY

The following example is based on records of an attempted major process innovation by Beta (a disguised name of a petrochemical manufacturer) over a seven-year period. This company's journey illustrates activities typically involved in both major and minor process innovations, though major innovations represent a longer, more costly, and potentially more profitable undertaking.

Beta's goal, which never changed, was to develop a new process to manufacture monomer A (a disguised name). During the seven years, Beta's activities were confined to applied research, the preparation of basic specifications, and the construction and operation of a pilot plant.

Beta's journey started when a senior organic chemist, in search of a major process innovation, identified a possible new process that might be used to manufacture monomer A. The instigation of a formal project required only the approval of the head of the corporate research and development department, which was responsible for developing new business lines.

Beta's goal was clearly stated: "Develop a new process for [monomer A] that will result in a commanding cost position compared to present commercial processes." Beta's researchers dreamed of a breakthrough so important that all existing plants would be shut down and replaced by new ones utilizing the technology. But even if plants with existing technology had sufficiently low marginal costs to continue operating, Beta could still earn handsome profits if the new technology were used by one or more of the new facilities that Beta believed would be needed in the future to meet normal growth for monomer A.

The possible process route identified by Beta's organic chemist had substantial advantages over the conventional process: lower-cost raw materials, smaller quantities of by-products, no toxic substances involved, and one reaction step instead of two.

During year seven, Beta reached an agreement with a European producer of monomer A under which the producer made a lump sum payment to Beta equivalent to about 10 percent of the $13 million Beta had spent on the project; the producer also agreed to build and operate a semicommercial unit, with a start-up scheduled for the beginning of year nine. If the semicommercial unit was successful, then the European producer was obligated to design, build, and operate a commercial unit in Europe—provided there was a market for the product. The plant would cost approximately $60 million and yield Beta $2 million yearly in royalties. Beta would be free to commercialize the technology elsewhere, including the United States and Japan, and expected to receive about $4 million yearly from each sale of technology.

In addition, Beta had been allowed eight U.S. and six foreign patents and had 25 U.S. and 113 foreign applications still pending. These patents and applications would not only help protect Beta's position in monomer A, but also might be of use to Beta in subsequent research and might generate fees from other companies.[7]

The following description of Beta's journey highlights two important factors, both of which were mentioned earlier in this chapter as crucial in developing new products: the reduction of uncertainty and the use of a communications network.

Reduction of Uncertainty

As with product innovation, it is convenient to classify the underlying causes of uncertainty into two categories: market and technology. Beta's researchers directed their major effort toward the technology issues, especially the conversion and yield of the reaction, the two items that have the greatest effect on investment and manufacturing costs of a new plant. Conversion, the portion of the raw materials that actually undergoes reaction, is important because of the high costs involved in separating unreacted raw materials from the product. Yield, the portion of the raw materials that ends up as a prime product rather than a low-value by-product or waste, is important because it affects raw-material costs. This focus on reactions naturally led to an intensive study of catalysts, which are used extensively in the petrochemical industry to facilitate reactions (see Table 3-2).

There are complex interactions, as well as trade-offs, between the variables that affect the reaction. For example, Beta researchers found that lowering the reaction temperature from 700°C to

Table 3-2
Examples of Technical Options Affecting Chemical Reactions in Beta's
Attempt to Develop a New Petrochemical Process

Catalyst Properties

Composition

Chemical reproducibility

Metals migration

Particle type

Particle size

Attrition characteristics and resistance

Mechanism of reaction

Sensitivity to poisoning

Reaction Conditions Directly Relating to Catalysts

Ratio of catalyst to raw material

Quantity of catalyst recycled

Method of regenerating catalyst

Surface area of catalyst

Type of catalyst bed: fluid versus fixed; packed bed versus fixed shell and
    tube

Dimensions of catalyst bed, including length and diameter of any tubes

Pressure drop across catalyst bed

Degree to which partially reduced state used

Degree to which catalyst doped with promoters

Other Reaction Conditions

Temperature

Pressure

State: anhydrous versus aqueous

Water versus steam

Ratio of steam to raw material

Batch versus continuous flow

Mode of entry and mixing of raw material

Time of reaction

Source: Beta's records.

550°C enabled them to use an inexpensive reactor with the catalyst packed onto a bed without tubes instead of an expensive reactor with tubes. And Beta's researchers examined a trade-off between a reaction with an 80 percent conversion and a 45 percent yield and a reaction with a 60 percent conversion and a 60 percent yield.

In spite of the large number of variables and almost infinitely large number of possible interactions, Beta's researchers proceeded systematically to reduce uncertainties. At the beginning of the project the two key goals selected were an 80 percent conversion and a 70 percent yield. During the second year, after extensive laboratory tests of different types of catalysts with varying properties under different reaction conditions, the researchers achieved a 70 percent conversion and 60 percent yield. Even though these results were short of the final goals, Beta researchers considered them satisfactory enough to begin scaling up the experiments to bench scale. This involved a continuous operation with a throughput of five pounds per hour. They continued to test a number of different catalysts under varying conditions. During year five, Beta placed in service a pilot plant, which had a capacity of 25 pounds per hour. But even with the pilot plant in operation, Beta continued parallel experiments on the bench-scale unit in order to obtain data on catalyst life and regeneration.

At the end of year six, when Beta brought the technical work in the R&D laboratory to a conclusion, the achievements had exceeded the goals for conversion and yield. For example, the conversion achieved was 82 percent versus the 80 percent goal, while the yield achieved was 73 percent versus the 70 percent goal. Moreover, the catalyst selected for use in a commercial plant had exhibited very satisfactory performance by functioning successfully for more than one year, with regeneration possible while the unit was in operation.

Although Beta's researchers focused the overwhelming share of their efforts on reducing technical uncertainty, they were monitoring the market picture as well. On the surface, market uncertainty seemed low because of the clearly identified need of existing and new manufacturers for a lower-cost process for making monomer A. Monomer A, indeed, was a juicy target, and one easily identified. The potential market for a major process innovation was large and growing. Annual world output of monomer A was valued at over $1 billion. Most of the product was sold to nonintegrated polymer manufacturers; the remainder was used internally by the monomer manufacturers.

If Beta should be successful in developing a commercial process, it could, of course, build its own manufacturing facilities to use the process. The quality of monomer A was sufficiently standardized so that price would determine which firm made a sale. Early in the life of the project, the researchers estimated that the value of the technology in their own facility would be several million dollars annually.

In addition, each of the existing manufacturers of monomer A would be a potential purchaser of the process. The purchasers were easily identified because there were only two dozen or so in the world, and all were well-known petrochemical firms headquartered in major industrialized nations. Researchers estimated that a single sale of technology might generate at least several million dollars of royalties annually, and put the minimum total profit potential from technology sales at $10 million annually. Thus, Beta's researchers estimated that the total profit potential of a successful process innovation was at least $12 million annually.

Under this placid surface, however, there lurked a variety of complications. The key market uncertainty was the amount of productive capacity that might be built using Beta's technology. Beta defined its only explicit economic goal in terms of competing in the market for technology to be used in a new plant. The original cost goal was defined in terms of a target price: that is, a price at which the product could be sold and earn a return on investment of 20 percent. Beta's target price for its monomer A process was 25 cents per pound, about 30 percent lower than the price that Beta estimated would be required for a new plant using the conventional process, and 20 percent lower than the price required for new processes being developed by others. In year seven, Beta researchers believed that this goal of a target price of 25 cents would be met in a commercial plant. Beta's researchers used two different measures of market potential: the total yearly production of monomer A and the expected growth in consumption of monomer A.

The total annual production of monomer A exceeded one billion pounds in the United States and two billion pounds abroad at the time when the project began. To capture this market, Beta's new process would have to be used in new facilities that would replace existing capacity. For such a use, the *total costs*—including a return on the new investment—of product from a new plant using Beta's technology would have to be lower than the *marginal costs* of keeping an existing plant operating, but without the necessity of earning a return on the existing investment. For example, if Beta could sell monomer A for 25 cents a pound and earn an adequate profit in a facility using its new technology, existing plants with a marginal cost above 25 cents per pound eventually would be forced to shut down. In actual fact, the marginal cost of the existing facilities was lower than 25 cents, thereby depriving Beta of the market served by the existing facilities.

Beta's other measure of market potential—the growth rate for consumption—would determine the amount of the new capacity needed. At the start of the project, the researchers believed that new capacity, in the form of a new plant, would be needed within five years and that, subsequently, additional capacity would be needed on a regular basis. Thus, an adequate market seemed to be available, since Beta's original goal was to develop a new process and build a new commercial plant in five years. The investment cost of removing capacity bottlenecks in existing plants proved to be quite low, however, so considerable additional capacity was added by this route. This development, therefore, extended the time during which new capacity would not be needed—to perhaps eleven or twelve years rather than five years from the time the project was started. In fact, the delay to year eleven or twelve might not result in any postponement, or at least not much of one, of commercialization since year ten or eleven was the earliest time when new capacity of a commercial scale could be available from Beta's licensee. Beta's licensee, of course, had to build and operate a semicommercial plant before it could build a commercial-scale facility.

Thus, at the end of year seven, Beta faced two important uncertainties. Would the operation of the semicommercial plant indicate that a commercial plant using Beta's technology could make monomer A at a lower cost than competing processes? When would capacity from a new commercial plant be needed?

Communications Links

Throughout the journey, communications on the monomer A project took place principally within Beta's research and development department. A person in the organic chemistry section of this department started the project. Subsequently, members of the process research, catalyst, and pilot plant sections became involved. The head of the team was a member of the process research section. The director of research at Beta was ultimately responsible for the project, although overall funding for the total R&D budget was determined by the president.

Prime responsibility for the project always rested with the research and development team, which obtained assistance from others inside Beta. For example, the patent attorney began to file patents in year two. Beginning in year four, the R&D team went to three other organizations within Beta: the licensing group for suggestions of possible licensing targets, the engineering department for the design of the off-site facilities for a pilot plant and for aid in designing a commercial plant, and the business development group for a critique of an evaluation of the project by an outside engineering company. In year five, the researchers asked a manufacturing plant manager within the company for information about the possibility of locating a new monomer facility at the manager's plant. These contacts were sporadic and took place primarily only between the R&D team and other organizations, rather than being contacts among the other organizations.

It was also the research staff who conducted the principal contacts outside Beta, the most numerous being potential customers for the technology, who were also manufacturers of monomer A and hence potential competitors. The R&D team contacted only 23 outside organizations over a seven-year period (see Table 3-3).

It is noticeable that process innovation has certain key features in common with product innovation. First, basic research, which is usually not done by the innovator, provides the foundation of knowledge on which the process innovation is built. Second, the reduction of uncertainty is a central feature of process innovation, just as it is for product innovation. But a closer analysis reveals substantial differences between the two types of innovation.

Table 3-3

Contacts outside Beta by Beta's Research Department

	Individual Organizations Contacted		
Type of Organization	Number	When	Purpose of Contact
Potential customers and competitors	11	years 3–7	Discuss possibility of joint effort to develop the technology
Consultants	4	years 1 and 4	Obtain research assistance on catalysts and corrosion; obtain market study
Custom manufacturers	0		
Testing laboratories	0		
Engineering firms	4	years 4 and 5	Select one large firm to provide engineering services during process development and ultimately to design and construct commercial plant; select a small firm to provide specialized design services
Others, including raw-material suppliers	4	years 3 and 5	Obtain equipment and catalysts
Total organizations contacted	23		

Source: Beta's records.

ALPHA, BETA, AND MODELS OF INNOVATION

Any conclusions drawn from only two cases, even if their activities are believed to be typical for the whole petrochemical industry, must be considered tentative. Thus, any deductions based on the analysis below should be considered more as hypotheses for further testing rather than as concrete findings. With this limitation in mind, Alpha and Beta's experiences are compared with earlier models of innovation and with each other. As suggested at the outset of this chapter, Alpha's experience with product innovation and Beta's with process innovation suggest that, at least in the case of petrochemicals, specific modifications in prior models of innovation are necessary.

The traditional concept of innovation from which the Alpha and Beta cases depart is the idea of a simple linear progression from one step to another. These steps are (1) generation of an idea, (2) screening, (3) business analysis, (4) development, (5) testing, and (6) commercialization.[8] In fact, because of *recycling* and *simultaneity,* this conventional model is quite inadequate in describing the real world.

There is a large amount of recycling from "later" stages back to "earlier" ones. One example from Alpha was that after the testing of baked-on coatings (step 5, "testing," in the conventional model), Alpha carried out additional screening (step 2) and business analysis (step 3). Then Alpha researchers generated a new idea (step 1) in trying nonbaked coatings. Furthermore, in reality, a number of steps are often conducted simultaneously. For example, Alpha researchers, when considering flexible foams, were screening (step 2), analyzing business opportunities (step 3), developing and improving the process (step 4), and testing potential applications (step 5), all at the same time.

Given that Alpha managers considered *seven* different target markets to be served by *four* different types of polymers made from *nine* different intermediate monomers, in turn made from *dozens* of different raw materials via *twenty* different processes, it is not surprising that the amount of recycling and simultaneity among the six steps was enormous.

In contrast, Beta did much less recycling than Alpha did. Beta researchers, by and large, started with one set of ideas and proceeded to march through the first three steps quickly, working most of the time on the *development* of the process and the *testing* of catalysts and different reaction conditions. True, at a lower level of detail, such as testing catalysts, new ideas were generated and then carried through the various steps. Simultaneity was prevalent in Beta's case, especially in the activities of *business analysis, development,* and *testing.* Still, there was less simultaneity in Beta's than in Alpha's case.

Thus, although the conventional model of innovation based on a simple linear progression is not fully adequate in describing Beta's attempt to develop a new process, it seems more applicable to Beta than to Alpha's attempted product innovation.

The second traditional concept of innovation that might need revision is the often accepted research categorization as either "demand-pull" or "technology-push." In the case of Alpha, a research scientist did initiate the idea, but he had in mind a possible market, and there was plenty of market feedback that generated new ideas. Hence, some observers might characterize the project as "technology-push" with a strong check by marketing. In fact, a better description is that it involved "backing and forthing" between demand and supply considerations.[9]

This "backing and forthing" highlights the amount of uncertainty inherent in innovation at the levels of both the individual project and R&D project selection. Indeed, in Alpha's case, it is difficult to define whether there was just one project or many, or, if there were more than one, how many there were.

Like the Alpha case, Beta's journey illustrates the difficulty of distinguishing between "demand-pull" and "technology-push" as the driving force behind an innovation. As at Alpha, it was a scientist at Beta who had the initial idea, but he, too, did have in mind a possible market. On the other hand, Beta did much less "backing and forthing" between demand and supply considerations than did Alpha. Furthermore, the boundaries of Beta's project were quite clear.

Still, "backing and forthing," combined at times with the difficulty of defining the boundaries of a project, means that a third model of innovation perhaps needs revision—the idea of the innovator as a profit maximizer. True, researchers may have profit maximization as a goal, but as Nelson and Winter point out, the term *maximizing profits* is grossly inadequate in describing the activities of R&D managers, either when they are taking action on a project or selecting a set of projects. Rather, they are engaged in search processes that interact and they aim primarily at goals that are near rather than ultimate. Moreover, instead of comprehensive analyses implied by profit maximization, they often use rules of thumb to guide their decisions.[10]

In spite of much trial and error in testing catalysts and reaction conditions, overall, Beta's choices were more limited than Alpha's and the company faced less uncertainty than did Alpha. Hence, Beta was more able to aim clearly at an ultimate goal. In this sense, Beta's behavior more clearly fits the traditional concept of "profit maximization" than did that of Alpha, which was engaged more heavily in interacting search processes.

A fourth area in which ideas in the literature might need modification involves process innovation. Nelson and Winter state that process improvements likely come from the R&D done by suppliers and embodied in their products.[11] This description hardly fits petrochemicals. Most new processes have been developed by petrochemical manufacturers rather than suppliers, and Beta's case illustrates that most of the effort involves resources within the firm.

True, some processes are innovated by engineering firms, and an innovation represents a product of the firm. In such a case, however, the supplier would be a supplier of knowledge rather than of equipment. It is also true that several engineering contractors—Foster Wheeler, for example—manufacture certain pieces of equipment, but the equipment and process design are sold as separate products, the sale of one not being dependent on the other.[12]

On the other hand, Alpha and Beta more or less match some models of innovation found in the literature. For example, William Abernathy and James Utterback, using studies at the Harvard Business School, stated that when faced with uncertainty in both market and technology, the decision maker has little incentive for major investments in formal R&D because of the high risk involved. The authors went on to state that as uncertainty is reduced, there is greater incentive and hence higher spending on R&D, at least until later in the product's life, when R&D expenditures decline. This decline is said to occur because by then firms are using costly specialized production processes, thereby making the cost of implementing technological innovation prohibitively high. Furthermore, increasing price competition erodes profits with which to fund R&D.[13]

Although most features of this picture seem to fit the petrochemical industry, some do not. For example, during Alpha's nine-year journey, uncertainty was very high about both markets and technology, and Alpha's level of expenditures was low compared with what would be required if the project proceeded. Indeed, consistent with Abernathy and Utterback's findings, Alpha never reduced uncertainty enough to make the major investment required for a pilot plant. If Alpha had developed a product such that market uncertainty was sufficiently low, it would have built a pilot plant and incurred substantial expenses in operating it in order to reduce market, as well as technical, uncertainty further. Beta perceived much less market uncertainty than Alpha and did build a pilot plant. Also consistent with Abernathy and Utterback's results are the aggregate data in chapter 2 on petrochemical process innovation (see Figure 2-1), which suggest that firms do not continue to increase their expenditures in R&D as a product gets older. But the reasons for this apparent fall in R&D spending after the third decade of a petrochemical's life are not those advanced by Abernathy and Utterback—increasing specialization of the production process and lower profits with which to fund R&D. The production facility to make a petrochemical is usually specialized at the time when the original commercial unit is built. Furthermore, companies in the petrochemical industry usually have a number of product lines and therefore are not dependent on the profitability of any single product to fund R&D. Rather, the number of new petrochemical processes developed, including both major and minor innovations, drops off in the latter years of a product's life, presumably because there is less chance of a profitable innovation.

The Alpha case supports existing literature concerning the importance of environmental factors in product innovation. First, it illustrates the necessity of close contact with the market, an idea that is an essential part of innovation theory. Second, Alpha illustrates the importance of being able to rely on a diverse group of suppliers while a technology is in a fluid state.[14] Alpha's case shows not only the importance of suppliers of goods, which is emphasized in conventional theory, but also the importance of the suppliers of services. Alpha obtained services from nine consultants, two custom manufacturers, four testing laboratories, and one engineering firm.

Obtaining information, goods, and services from outside the firm seems to be less important in process development than in product development. Whereas the Alpha group had contacts with more than 150 organizations outside the firm, Beta had contacts with only 23 external organizations. Furthermore, Alpha's contacts began earlier in the life of its project and were much more regular. The difference in the number of market contacts is particularly striking, as Alpha got in touch with more than 109 potential customers and competitors, compared with Beta's 11. The market for Alpha's product innovation was uncertain; hence, they had to search out many potential customers, whereas Beta had far fewer contacts because potential customers were limited and easily identified. Beta's task was also made easier by the fact that its communications with potential customers were more sporadic than Alpha's since there was no need to work with these customers on product testing. Hence, it appears that the marketing tasks facing a process innovator are much simpler than those facing a product innovator. On the other hand, Beta's task was complicated by the fact that 8 of the 11 potential customers were located abroad. Alpha felt no need to contact foreign firms because there were numerous potential customers in the large U.S. market.

Thus, product innovators, because they work very closely with many customers, seem more likely to depend on the domestic market than a foreign market, whereas process innovators, without the need for such close market contact and with fewer potential customers, can easily target foreign customers as well as domestic ones. This difference between product innovators and process innovators can affect where innovation occurs and who innovates.

CHAPTER 4

WHO INNOVATES AND WHERE

Where innovation takes place and who carries it out are important issues. Innovation helps create high income for nations in which it occurs and helps create monopoly profits for firms who do it.[1] The experiences of Alpha and Beta, data on the nine products, and other studies help illuminate these issues.

WHERE INNOVATION OCCURS

If one were to consider only input costs, one might suppose that R&D activity in petrochemicals would take place in a country with low costs for R&D personnel and facilities—Israel, for example. One line of argument as to why this has not occurred goes as follows. Although the firm that initially commercializes a product must consider the prices of existing products that compete with the new one, its customers are often not very sensitive to the new product's price because of the product's unique properties. As a result of this price insensitivity, the firm tends both to perform R&D and to locate its first commercial plant in a country with a market for the product because it has no particular incentive to look outside where costs might be lower.[2]

But even if a firm were to make a thorough search of costs in other countries, it might still reach the conclusion that other factors, especially those that aid in improving communications and reducing uncertainty, are important in considering where to conduct petrochemical innovation. This is not to say that a supply of R&D personnel and facilities does not matter, for it is obviously a necessary requirement for innovation. Good universities that can provide a ready supply of scientific and technical graduates are important.[3] Other factors, however, seem to overshadow the costs of R&D personnel and facilities.

Product Innovation

A body of research explains why innovation of new products—not just petrochemicals—tends to occur in large-market countries: that is, those with large populations and high incomes.[4] In fact, although the literature emphasizes the market size of the country in which product innovation occurs, market size per se does not tell the whole story. To be sure, the proximity of innovative activities to customers does matter, but so does proximity to suppliers and to the top management and operations of the firm undertaking the research.

The Alpha case illustrates the finding that applied research and development leading to product innovation require considerable communication between the firm's innovation specialists and its potential customers. The link between the marketing specialists and the customers is obvious, but, in addition, there is contact between the customers and the R&D people who produce samples. These two sets of contacts involved 59 different firms in Alpha's case. In petrochemicals, the typical customers are manufacturers of petrochemicals or their derivatives. There are more such customers in large-market countries because they have tended to locate their manufacturing facilities near the end markets rather than in countries that might have lower-cost materials or labor. Close proximity obviously aids communications.

Two other factors are also important. Within the country there usually are a number of outside specialists likely to know their home market. And materials suitable for manufacturing products for that market usually are available there. The reader might recall that Alpha, for example, had contact with more than 41 outside suppliers of goods and services. Such suppliers, of course, are more likely to be found in industrialized countries than in less developed areas.

Within the firm, the great uncertainty involved in applied research and development creates a need for managerial decisions at key points. Recall that Alpha's researchers required approval from general management on ten separate occasions to proceed with the project. Because good communication links aid such decisions, innovation specialists are likely to be located in the same country, and often the same metropolitan area, as general management. For example, immediately after World War I, many chemical companies set up R&D facilities in New Jersey in order to be near their national headquarters in the New York City area.[5] (An exception to this tendency is that pilot plants are sometimes located near large chemical plants or refineries so as to have an on-site source of various raw materials. Exxon's petrochemical pilot plants at its Baton Rouge refinery are an example.)

The need for good communication links also affects the location of the first commercial plant. The operators of the plant must communicate frequently with R&D personnel, general management, customers, and suppliers. Furthermore, it is efficient to have R&D people readily available to form the nucleus of the commercial plant's work force, at least during the early period of operation. International transfer of technology between R&D and commercial operations is especially costly because of long distances and differences in customs and language.[6]

The need for good communications between plant personnel and customers is especially important in solid petrochemicals such as polymers, elastomers, and fibers, because the products must meet a host of specifications. In polymers, for example, these can include impact resistance, durability, stability, weathering, set time, adhesion, flexibility, gloss, appearance, hardness, light stability, and resistance to abrasion and acid. Product improvement efforts and discussions with customers continue throughout the life cycle of solid petrochemicals, although more of them occur earlier in the life of a product than later.

Those petrochemicals that are gases or liquids, of course, generally have fewer characteristics that are important to customers. Purity is the primary criterion, since minor impurities in a monomer can harm the quality of any material made from it. Gaseous and liquid petrochemicals reach a standardized specification earlier in their lives than do solid petrochemicals. Even in the case of gases and liquids, however, there is still much negotiation—particularly about impurities—between the manufacturer and customers about product quality for some time after the initial commercial plant has been built.[7]

In general, such negotiations result in high marketing costs for new chemical products. According to one estimate, these costs average about 23 percent of the sales price during the introductory phase and decline to about 2 percent of it as a product reaches maturity.[8] There is every reason to believe that marketing costs of petrochemicals follow a similar path. Locating the initial commercial plant in a country with a large market not only makes the marketing effort more effective but also minimizes the early marketing costs by facilitating communications between the plant and the customers.

The desire to avoid risk, as well as to ensure good communications, reinforces the tendency to locate the first commercial plant in a large-market country. The large economies of scale in petrochemical manufacture set a lower limit on the size of the plant. Placing the plant in a country with a large market avoids the risk of depending on exports for a large percentage of the plant's output. An export market is more risky than the domestic market because of the possibility that the importing nation could erect trade barriers to protect producers of a competing product, or protect a firm that may in the future manufacture the product. Furthermore, there is quite a bit of evidence suggesting that executives—even in multinational enterprises—prefer to manufacture in their home country because of the risks inherent in operating abroad.[9]

The key communication links in the innovation process are shown in Figure 4-1. This is a highly simplified diagram since each link represents many individual communication paths. For example, the single link connecting the network of product-innovation specialists to customers can represent dozens of actual communication links, for a number of different specialists may be in contact with any given customer and there may be many customers.

The need for good communications and the desire to reduce uncertainty give large-market, industrialized countries containing

Figure 4-1
Communication Web Required for Innovation of New Petrochemical Products, within and outside the Innovating Firm (Simplified)

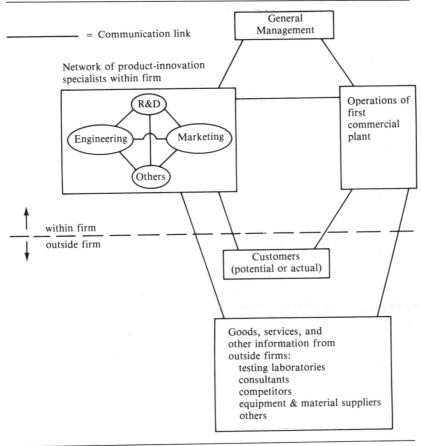

corporate headquarters a decided advantage over other countries for the location of product innovation in petrochemicals. Each of the nine products, as well as the 53 most important plastics, synthetic fibers, and synthetic rubbers, was produced initially in the country where the original commercializer had R&D facilities and its headquarters. Furthermore, all nine products were first manufactured commercially in prewar Germany or in the United States, the two countries with the largest domestic markets when the products were introduced. The first five were commercialized in

Germany because of that country's early lead in organic chemicals and plastics; the last four, in the United States during and after World War II. And 46 of the 53 most important plastics, synthetic fibers, and synthetic rubbers were first manufactured commercially in either the United States or Germany. The United Kingdom, France, and Italy accounted for six of the remaining seven.[10]

To be sure, the five countries also had a ready supply of scientific and technical graduates from good universities, but other countries that had good universities and small markets—Belgium and Switzerland, for example—were not homes of petrochemical product innovation. Thus, large markets seem to be important in explaining the location of product innovation in petrochemicals.

Process Innovation

Location in a large-market, industrialized country is also useful for a process innovator since the innovator might want to sell the technology and might need to purchase inputs. Still, compared with a product innovator, a process innovator has far fewer contacts with the market and needs a smaller variety and number of inputs from suppliers. Recall that Alpha had contacts with more than 150 organizations outside the firm, compared with Beta's 23, and of Beta's 11 contacts with potential customers, 8 were located outside its home country. Thus, the advantage that large-market countries have over small-market countries is smaller in process innovation than in product innovation. It is not surprising that while all nine products were innovated in the United States and prewar Germany, the two largest-market countries, only 54 percent of the 180 new processes subsequently commercialized to manufacture the nine products were developed in these two countries. While each of the first plants for the nine products was built in the product innovator's home country, 25 percent of the first plants to use one of the 180 process innovations were built outside the process innovator's home country.

Even though process innovators seem to need fewer supplies of goods and services than product innovators (Alpha's more than 41 versus Beta's 12), an industrial infrastructure seems to be very important in aiding process innovation. Only one of the 180 process innovations for the nine products occurred in a less-developed country. Other information indicates the lack of petrochemical know-how in such countries. In a 1977 survey of contemporary petrochemical projects, for example, only 8 of the 580 engineering and construction firms involved in some phase of the project were headquartered in less-developed countries and only one of the 223 exports of engineering and construction services was made by a firm headquartered in a less-developed country.[11] Even these meager beginnings of petrochemical-related know-how in less-developed countries were concentrated in the older engineering fields, especially civil, and to a lesser extent, mechanical engineering. The development of process technology, which relies heavily on chemical engineering—a newer field than civil or mechanical engineering—had barely begun in less-developed countries.

WHO INNOVATES

There is no generally accepted theory about the relationship between the size of a firm and its level of innovation, but there has been a long-running argument on the subject. Some authors say that the stultifying effects of large size outweigh its advantages; others maintain the opposite view.[12] The arguments about the advantages of size in the innovation process stem from Joseph Schumpeter and have been articulated well by Raymond Vernon, who stresses the roles of risk and communication.[13] Certain of Vernon's arguments apply to petrochemicals particularly.

Overall, the large firm seems to have an advantage because of risk-pooling, better reputation, superior resources, wider scope, and greater learning.

Risk-Pooling

As the Alpha and Beta cases illustrate, there is substantial risk associated with the long-term, large expenditures needed to commercialize a new petrochemical. Included in the risk is the cost of specialized personnel and equipment. Hiring highly skilled persons can be considered an investment decision because the firm is willing to take a negative return initially on specialists in order to receive a positive return later. The sums involved are not trivial;

the investment value of scientists, engineers, and general managers in the eight most skill-oriented U.S. industries is equivalent to about 30 percent of the net worth of the firms. (Although petrochemicals are part of one of the eight industries—the chemical industry—the capital-intensiveness of petrochemicals means that the figure for petrochemicals is lower than 30 percent; but it is still important.) Moreover, hiring skilled workers is risky because the firm may have misestimated and not have sufficient need for them, the workers may not perform up to expectations, or they may leave or die.[14]

Even if small firms in the aggregate have the same record of research successes, and hence the same return of profit on their R&D investment, as large firms, the latter would still have an advantage. Given the plausible assumption that a large firm will start more projects than a small firm will, the proportion of successes for a single large firm is more closely predictable than that for a single small firm. The greater predictability, of course, means lower risk for the same return, a condition preferred by investors.

Better Reputation

The desire on the part of prospective users to avoid risk causes them to favor large firms as suppliers of a new product or process. Du Pont, for example, is seen as a more reliable supplier than a small, and perhaps unknown, chemical company. Even if this were not the case, the customer's executive responsible for the purchase is less likely to have problems with other executives at the customer's own firm if Du Pont, rather than the small, unknown company, fails to deliver a quality product or process.[15]

Superior Resources

The large economies of scale in the commercial manufacture of petrochemicals favor large firms. The cost of a plant of minimum economic size represents a relatively larger risk for small companies than for large ones.[16] The risk is made even greater by the specialized nature of many petrochemical plants; a plant usually cannot be converted to produce other chemicals if the new product proves to be unprofitable. Of course, a small firm could develop the product or process and then, rather than build a commercial facility, could sell the technology to a large firm for commercialization. There is some impediment to doing this in the petrochemical industry because the market for knowledge is notably imperfect—more about this in chapter 6.[17]

Wider Scope

Another major advantage possessed by large firms relates to efficient communications. There are advantages for a firm to have within itself the specialists and specialized equipment needed for product innovation:

- a high degree of secrecy is involved, and secrets are easier to keep if outsiders are not present;
- face-to-face communication is the major way to exchange information and is typically easier within a firm than across firms;
- most persons involved in innovation—the minority of scientists being an exception—are more receptive to signals received from within their firms than from outside; and
- the specialists and specialized equipment will be more readily available if located within the firm rather than being hired and purchased as needed.[18]

Firms do rely on outside assistance for R&D, but large companies are more likely to have within the firm certain specialists and equipment, because large programs can keep such specialists and equipment occupied, whereas small programs cannot.

Alpha's case provides insight into the types of activity that are contracted to outsiders. In general, Alpha used outsiders for very specialized information or services that Alpha could not generate economically within the firm. For example, Alpha obtained from consulting firms studies of existing markets and available technology with which Alpha personnel were not familiar. In addition to purchasing information, Alpha had products tested by outside laboratories that specialized in testing building materials and polymers. Alpha also had limited quantities of products made by custom manufacturers that had equipment of the appropriate size.

The tasks for which Alpha contracted with outsiders had two

characteristics in addition to being specialized. First, they were sufficiently well defined so that a price for the service could readily be determined. Second, they were not the heart of the innovation. Although the innovation would represent the result of a large and varied set of activities, the heart of the innovation was the laboratory work for which proper manufacturing conditions and product specifications were sought. These activities remained within Alpha.

Scope also affects the use of knowledge generated in research. With its wider field of activities, the large firm is more likely to be able to find a commercial application for a research discovery.[19] The small firm could sell the knowledge, but, again, it would encounter the problem of the imperfect market.

Greater Learning

A final advantage of large firms is that their greater number of innovations compared with small firms results in lower introduction costs because of the greater experience obtained.[20]

Though the evidence cited supports the argument that large firms have an advantage over small firms in innovation in petrochemicals, the enormous body of economic literature on the relationship between the size of a firm and its level of innovation draws very few solid conclusions.[21] Furthermore, the relatively small proportion of it that deals explicitly with petrochemicals contains contradictory conclusions. Most evidence, however, tends to support the large-firm advantage for petrochemicals.[22]

Even though large firms might have an overall advantage in innovation in petrochemicals, there is a difference in the relative advantages of different-sized firms in product innovation compared with process innovation.

Product Innovation

The evidence clearly reveals that large firms have an advantage over small firms in petrochemical product innovation. A glance at the names of the first companies to begin commercial production of 13 principal classes of plastics reads like a page from *Who's*

Who in the world chemical industry, and most of these firms were well established long before the introduction of the plastic in question.[23] True, in a few cases, usually in the early decades of the industry, some companies came into existence to produce a single product. For example, General Bakelite, later merged into Union Carbide, came into existence in 1909 in order to commercialize phenol-formaldehyde resins.[24]

Relatively big firms introduced all of the nine products (see Table 4-1). Bayer and BASF were among the largest firms in the German chemical industry, and they and five other of the largest firms merged in 1925 to form I.G. Farben, which then dominated the German chemical industry. Likewise, in the United States, Du Pont was the largest chemical firm, Standard Oil of New Jersey the largest in petroleum, and Standard Oil of California was also an established giant in the petroleum industry.[25]

Process Innovation

Whereas large firms have been dominant in *product* innovation in the petrochemical industry, firms of various sizes have participated in *process* innovation. As in the case of product innovation, however, the size of the firm is important in process innovation. For example, the dramatic rise and fall of resources used on the monomer A project by Beta (see Figure 4-2) can be better handled by a large firm than a small one. On the other hand, the task facing even the early process innovators requires much less market development and hence, other things being equal, is less costly and risky than product innovation. For the nine products, the early process innovators—although relatively large firms—were smaller than the product innovators.

As new processes for the nine products became less radical in nature and as less market development was needed, the process innovators were smaller still. The three bars on the left side of Figure 4-3 show the relative sizes of product innovators and those process innovators that were primarily manufacturing companies. (As noted in Figure 4-3, engineering contractors were omitted from this analysis.)

Companies that purchase technology for use in their plants, in effect, play the role of manufacturing specialists. For any product

Table 4-1

Selected Information about Original Commercialization of Nine Products

Year of Initial Commercialization	Name of Product	Innovator (Firm that Initially Commercialized Product)	Nation in Which Innovator Headquartered	Nation in Which Product Initially Commercialized
1907	Synthetic phenol	Bayer	Germany	Germany
1923	Synthetic methanol	BASF	Germany	Germany
1927	Vinyl chloride monomer	Dynamit-Nobel (I.G. Farben)	Germany	Germany
1931	Styrene monomer	BASF (I.G. Farben)	Germany	Germany
1933	Acrylonitrile	BASF (I.G. Farben)	Germany	Germany
1942	Cyclohexane	Du Pont	United States	United States
1944	Isoprene	Standard Oil of New Jersey	United States	United States
1945	Orthoxylene	Standard Oil of California	United States	United States
1949	Paraxylene	Standard Oil of California	United States	United States

Source: Robert Stobaugh, "Creating a Monopoly: Product Innovation in Petrochemicals," in R. S. Rosenbloom, ed., Research on Technological Innovation, Management and Policy (Greenwich, CT: JAI Press, Inc., 1985), p. 99.

Figure 4-2
Annual Resources Used by Beta in Development of Process for
Monomer A

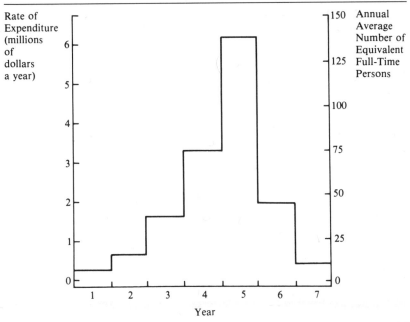

Sources: Company records.

for which they buy technology, they usually need no process research and little technical service, and if the product is a commodity, they need no market development. They do, of course, need a
marketing organization, but marketing expenses are very low for
the mature products, which are often the ones made with purchased technology. The lack of elaborate overhead is reflected in
the size of technology purchasers. For example, the companies
that bought technology to manufacture one of the nine products
were generally smaller than manufacturing companies that developed their own technology.

To be sure, many companies, especially the large ones, play a
number of different roles within the petrochemical industry,
adopting different strategies for various product lines. For example, they develop some products, innovate some processes early
and others late, and purchase still other processes.

Figure 4-3
Relative Sizes of Manufacturing Companies that Developed or
Purchased Technology to Make Four Petrochemical Products, Year of
Commercial Introduction through 1974

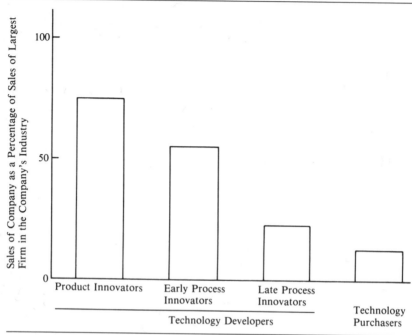

Notes: The products are the four of the nine products that were originally commercialized in the United States, see Table 4-1.

For each product, any firm that innovated a process in the first half of the period between the original commercialization of the product and 1974 was classified as an "early process innovator"; the other process innovators were classified as "late process innovators."

Engineering contractors, who rarely manufacture petrochemicals, were omitted because their activities are not comparable to those of manufacturing companies. The engineering contractors would be among the smaller manufacturing companies, or "technology purchasers," in terms of sales, and among the "late process innovators" in terms of when they introduced process innovations.

Sources: Industry trade journals, company annual reports, and author's questionnaire.

This picture contradicts two widely held views on competition within industries. One view is that the leader-follower role is crucial.[26] Actually, within the petrochemical industry, at any one time a company is both a leader and a follower, depending on the product. A second, and related view, is that the leaders stay ahead of subsequent entrants by grabbing an early lead. Only four of the product innovators of the nine products, however, still manufac-

Table 4-2

Industry Position in 1982 of Innovator of Each of Nine Products

Name of Product	Innovator	Year of Initial Commercialization	Original Innovator's Market Position in Home Country	Original Innovator's Market Share (percentage)		World Leader's Market Share (percentage)	
				Innovator's Home Country	World	World Leader's Home Country	World
Synthetic phenol	Bayer	1907	0	0%	0%	100%	9%
Synthetic methanol	BASF	1923	2 of 4	17	2	30	10
Vinyl chloride monomer	Dynamit-Nobel	1927	7 of 7	6	1	22	6
Styrene monomer	BASF	1931	1 of 3	44	5	21	14
Acrylonitrile	BASF	1933	0	0	0	44	26
Cyclohexane	Du Pont	1942	0	0	0	51	20
Isoprene	Standard Oil of New Jersey	1944	0	0	0	100	25
Orthoxylene	Standard Oil of California	1945	0	0	0	23	6
Paraxylene	Standard Oil of California	1949	7 of 10	7	3	39	18

Sources: Unpublished analysis by author and Harry Sachinis, Harvard Business School, 1983, based on industrial trade journals, plus correspondence with companies.

ture the product; of these, none is the world leader and only one
has the largest market share in its home country (see Table 4-2).
Presumably an important reason for the decline is that only one of
the innovators ever developed a new process for the product that it
originally commercialized.

In spite of the diversity of activities among different companies,
the general conclusion holds that product innovators, by and
large, are the biggest chemical and oil companies, followed in size
by early process innovators, late process innovators, and finally,
technology purchasers. The entry of these additional firms has a
substantial impact on profits.

CHAPTER 5

THE PROFIT SQUEEZE

Early in the life of a product, when there are few competitors, profit levels are high. But, as previous chapters have demonstrated, technological changes in the form of major and minor process innovations allow additional competitors to enter the field. As the number of producers increases, price cuts cause profit levels to decline and eventually to reach a level just high enough to attract needed capacity. At this stage, the high level of profits due to the existence of few competitors—that is, oligopolistic profits—are low or nonexistent.

Increased competition is not the only force that affects prices. Also at work are the other forces, identified in chapter 2, that companies use in their attempts to maintain or increase profits over the life of a product—product modifications, process improvements, and larger-sized plants.

Figure 5-1 shows the combined effects of these factors on the price of a petrochemical. In this idealized model, two factors cause a price decline by narrowing the profit margin—the increase in the number of competitors and the increase in product standardization caused by the lessening of opportunities for product modifications as a product's technology matures. The decline in profit margin is shown as the shaded area in Figure 5-1: that is, the difference between the unit price and unit cost. The other two factors—process improvements and large-sized plants—result in lower operating costs, the savings from which are passed through to consumers in the form of a lower unit price.

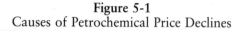

Figure 5-1
Causes of Petrochemical Price Declines

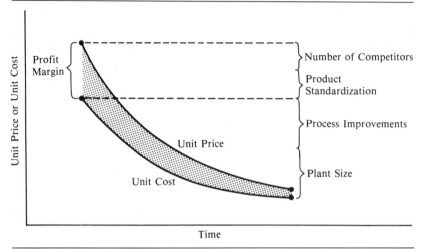

Source: Robert B. Stobaugh and Phillip L. Townsend, "Price Forecasting and Strategic Planning: The Case of Petrochemicals," *Journal of Marketing Research,* February 1975, p. 20.

This model assumes that the costs of the basic raw materials change relatively little in real terms, which was indeed the situation up until the early 1970s. After 1972 petrochemical prices rose dramatically. The rise was due in part to general inflation, which drove up operating costs and the cost of building new plants, but most of it was caused by the dramatic increase in the prices of oil and natural gas, which, of course, are the major raw materials and fuels used in the production of petrochemicals. Nevertheless, the forces shown in the model and explained in this chapter were still at work. (A statistical test of the model, using U.S. conditions for the 82 most commercially important petrochemicals, is available from the author.)[1]

Direct measures of profits on a given product are not easy to come by, for one would need to know a company's raw material, manufacturing, and other costs—information rarely available to outsiders. Given a set of reasonable assumptions, however, it is possible to impute a change in the level of profits—even though the exact level may not be known—by using changes in prices as an indicator of changes in profits.

Some idea of the magnitude of price declines can be obtained by a glance at Figure 5-2, which shows price indices through 1972 for eight of the nine products for which price data are available (these eight are also included in the sample of 82). Average yearly prices of each product moved down erratically, and in each case the price at the end of the period was substantially lower than in the year when the price was first available.

THE IMPACT OF ADDITIONAL COMPETITORS

The concept that the addition of competitors leads to lower profits is widely accepted, and studies have shown the existence of this pattern in the petrochemical industry. For example, two research-ers at Du Pont reported a decline in the profit on new products marketed by that firm, noting that when three to four producers existed, an oligopoly could no longer maintain substantial profit margins. And research at Harvard by Marvin Lieberman on 37 chemical products, including 26 petrochemicals, indicated that profits are higher for products when there are only five or so producers rather than many producers.[2] An investigation of styrene monomer demonstrates the decline in oligopoly profits as the level of competition increased (see Appendix E). This study serves mainly to illustrate the difficulty of determining changes in profit level associated with individual products, for the work was tedious, required a number of assumptions, and could not have been done with confidence by someone without business experi-ence with the product.[3]

Test results of the model that used U.S. conditions for the 82 most commercially important petrochemicals indicate that a change in the number of competitors was significant in explaining price changes over all of the time intervals studied, which were one, three, five, and seven years (all price changes were real in the sense that prices were corrected for inflation). Lieberman's work gives additional insight into the role of competition in affecting prices. He found that the entry of new competitors was important in explaining price declines. The effect of new competitors was especially strong when the firms came from a different industry, such as oil rather than chemicals.[4] The departure of firms has an

Figure 5-2

Price Index Trends in Constant Dollars for Eight Petrochemical
Products from Year of First Availability of Price through 1972

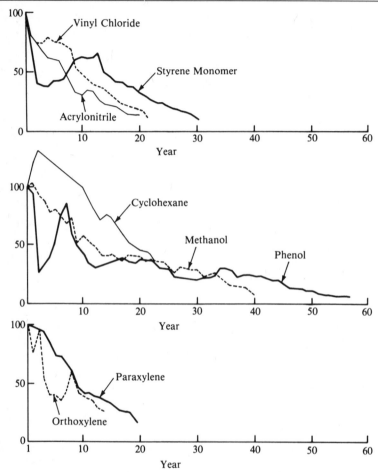

Note: Isoprene is not included because price data for this product were not available for a
sufficient number of years.
Source: Robert B. Stobaugh and Phillip L. Townsend, "Price Forecasting and Strategic
Planning: The Case of Petrochemicals," *Journal of Marketing Research,* February 1975, p.
21, and U.S. International Trade Commission, *Synthetic Organic Chemicals–U.S. Production and Sales* (Washington, DC: GPO), various years.

opposite effect: prices tend to stay higher than they would otherwise be.[5]

Of course, the intensity of competition, and hence prices, can be affected by other factors, such as the level of capacity utilization in the industry and marketing tactics. These factors, however, are generally short-term or cyclical aberrations upon the long-term pattern described in this chapter.[6]

THE IMPACT OF PRODUCT STANDARDIZATION

Product differentiation increases profits by reducing competition. In effect, a manufacturer who differentiates his or her product recreates a monopoly in a product by purposely making it slightly different from the standardized product sold by competitors. But when all producers offer products with the same specifications, it is difficult to compete by product differentiation. There can be some differences in the level of consumer service offered by different producers, but, in practice, producers of standardized products tend to compete on the basis of price. Maintaining monopoly or oligopoly profits is difficult. This finding is an important part of the product life-cycle concept, which holds that product standardization and price competition are characteristics acquired by products as they mature.[7]

There is no easy way to represent the degree of standardization of a petrochemical product, but for this purpose the 82 products were classified into two categories. The first contains products that have relatively standard specifications after a short introductory period; hence, users freely interchange products from different producers. Virtually all liquid and gaseous petrochemicals fall into this category. The second contains products that are subject to specification changes over most of their lifetime, and virtually all solid petrochemicals, such as polymers, fibers, and elastomers, are in this category.[8]

This measure was significant in explaining price declines over intervals of five and seven years, but not over one and three years. Presumably, the competitive effects of changing product quality take some time to operate, but, inevitably, products become more standardized and prices fall, because it becomes increasingly difficult to make additional significant technological changes in a product in order to differentiate it from those of competitors.[9]

THE IMPACT OF PROCESS IMPROVEMENTS

At the same time that profits are undermined by more competitors entering the field and competition stemming from product standardization, petrochemical firms attempt to maintain or increase profits by lowering production costs through technological improvements. Doing this results in a decline in production costs throughout the life of a product, a phenomenon often illustrated by the "experience curve" or "learning curve," first observed in the direct labor hours required for airframe manufacture prior to World War II. W. B. Hirschmann extended this concept to experience gains in oil and chemical processes, among others. He concluded that besides the savings in direct labor, broader categories of manufacturing costs declined in a regular way as cumulative production increased. In the late 1960s, the Boston Consulting Group began to promote the use of learning curves (which they called experience curves) in the formulation of corporate strategy. As a result of these and other studies, there is some confusion in what is meant by the learning curve. Here the term refers to any type of process improvement. Some studies of the learning curve use cumulative production as the only explanatory variable; hence, they automatically include as part of the learning phenomenon cost reductions resulting from bigger plants.[10]

In the case of existing plants, a process for making a given product undergoes continual improvements in efficiency. These cost-reducing improvements come in many forms, but generally involve increasing yield and conversion through technological improvements in catalysts and equipment and through the familiarity of the technical staff and operators with the equipment and the processes. Knowledge of these improvements, of course, can be used in new plants. But in the case of those new plants that use a new process (either major or minor process innovation), the learning curve—reflecting costs—is initially pushed down mainly by the knowledge embodied in the process innovation rather than by minor process improvements.

The usual statement on the effects of the learning curve is that "direct manufacturing cost decreases by a specified percentage as cumulative production doubles." As in the case of measuring profits, price is related to manufacturing cost, which is hard to determine because of the lack of published data. The study of the 82 products found that cumulated production experience in the United States was significant in explaining price declines over all four time intervals studied. Lieberman, too, found cumulated production experience to be significant in explaining price changes. In an analysis of related factors, he found that R&D expenditures tended to increase the steepness of the learning curve: that is, to accelerate the rate of learning.[11] Further, he found that the start-up of new plants, which he assumed embodied new technologies, was significant in causing price declines in highly competitive situations, although not in less competitive situations.[12] In three massive multiclient studies of competitive materials, Phillip Townsend (now a consultant, who was formerly at Harvard Business School) found that experience curves on a value-added basis existed for a sample of petrochemicals and polymers that are among the sample of the 82 products studied in this chapter.[13]

Note that all of these studies use cumulative production for the industry rather than for individual firms. This implies that information acquired through learning diffuses rapidly throughout the industry rather than being retained with the firm. To determine the extent to which such industrywide diffusion occurs, one would need data on cost and volume of production for individual firms, but such data are not available; hence, the industrywide data were used by necessity.

In fact, petrochemical firms go to great lengths to keep proprietary information from leaking to competitors. Union Carbide's petrochemical organization, for example, for years had a policy of not filing process patents, in an attempt to keep its operations highly secret—to the extent of calling its units by code names and calibrating its instruments so that the nontechnical plant operators would know neither the product they were making nor the operating conditions under which it was made. Technical personnel in overall charge of any given operation or responsible for process improvements, of course, would know. Monsanto, for example, has used code names in order to hide the identity of projects involving innovations. A number of firms post signs in their laboratories and operating units reminding personnel about the importance of secrecy. These efforts help explain why proprietary information in the chemical industry seems to leak out more slowly than in other industries. Edwin Mansfield found that chemical company executives believed that the detailed nature and operation of a new chemical process frequently could be kept secret for years. On the other hand, Lieberman, using an indirect statistical measure, could not find evidence that firms were able to keep information acquired through learning from diffusing rapidly throughout the industry, although he measured diffusion that was authorized (through licensing) as well as unauthorized.[14]

Undoubtedly firms in the petrochemical industry can keep some information secret for long periods of time, while other information leaks more quickly. The leaked information, combined with other factors that might be related to cumulative industry production such as developments by suppliers, causes the cumulative production of a product by the industry to be a variable that explains industrywide price declines for that product.

THE IMPACT OF LARGER PLANTS

The size of production facilities tends to increase over time as the size of the market grows and producers search for ways to gain a competitive advantage and boost profits by lowering their production costs. Assume that two petrochemical plants employ the same technology and both operate at full capacity. If plant A has an annual capacity of 100 units and plant B a capacity of 200 units, then plant B would be expected to have lower unit costs of production. For double the output, B would typically require only about 15 percent more operating labor and 50 percent more capital investment than A; in other words, at the same rate of capacity utilization, doubling the size of a plant would reduce unit costs for labor by 42 percent and capital-related items by 25 percent.[15] Although building larger plants is not in itself an example of technological innovation, larger plants are sometimes made economically feasible by technological innovation. For example, for one of the nine products, methanol, the development of large centrifugal compressors allowed large-scale plants to have a lower cost per unit of output than smaller plants.[16]

Over time, the benefits that can be obtained by building larger plants drop off because each doubling of plant size results in a smaller absolute reduction in unit costs. Beyond a certain point, the payoff from large plant size in some cases has not been enough to justify the additional investment. Operating one large plant rather than two smaller plants is riskier in several ways: capacity utilization might be lower because of reduced ability to match expansion timing to market growth, and a strike or explosion could eliminate a producer's only source of supply. In addition, cost savings from larger plants can be more than offset by additional transportation costs associated with shipping from one plant rather than two, since two plants can be located close to different intended markets. In practice, these factors as well as the size of the manufacturer's expected market have limited plants to a smaller size than pure engineering calculations might dictate. Still, the fact that the number of plants worldwide for many petrochemicals is relatively few (remember the Beta case) provides general support for the importance of plant size.

Plant size was found to be significant in explaining price changes over intervals of five to seven years, but not over one- and three-year intervals. Presumably, the change in average plant size over the shorter terms was too small to have a significant effect. But over extended periods of time the smaller plants—generally those built early-on by the product innovator and its competitors—become uneconomic and are closed as larger plants are brought onstream.[17]

STRATEGIC IMPLICATIONS FOR EARLY INNOVATORS

The ability to lower production costs through experience has an important impact on pricing strategy. For as A. Michael Spence of Harvard University has demonstrated, part of the firm's short-run marginal cost can be regarded as an investment that reduces the cost of production in future periods. Spence has shown that in the absence of competitors, a profit-maximizing firm lowers prices more slowly than costs, thereby causing short-run margins to widen as time passes. In fact, judgments about the possibility of the entry of competition play an important part in determining a pricing strategy.[18] In the early stages of the product's life, when there are few producers and profits are high, the oligopolists may adopt either of two basic strategies—the "high-price" and "low-price." The choice obviously depends, to an important extent, on a firm's belief about the degree to which it can keep proprietary information from being used by competitors, through a combination of patents and secrecy.

In adopting a high-price plan, the firms keep prices high in order to make substantial profits quickly. These firms realize that high prices and profits will encourage competitors to enter the business by innovating new processes. Further, this high-price strategy retards market growth to some extent.

Setting high prices seems to be the best strategy whenever the early oligopolists believe that other firms have basic business positions that will enable them to enter the market regardless of the pricing plan adopted by the early oligopolists. An example of this among the nine products is cyclohexane. Du Pont was its first producer, but the manufacture of cyclohexane is so closely integrated with the operations of an oil refinery that oil refiners have an inherent cost advantage over such companies as Du Pont, which did not have an oil refinery at that time. Du Pont eventually stopped manufacturing the product and only oil refiners were left in the cyclohexane business.

Alternatively, the high-price strategy would be desirable if the oligopolists thought their basic position was so strong that others could not enter even if prices and profits were kept high. This does not seem a realistic view for petrochemicals except in the very rare case where economically viable process technology is so well covered with patents that others could not commercialize new processes. This has not, however, occurred for any of the nine products.

In adopting a low-price strategy, firms cut prices to match or exceed cost reductions, in the hope that low prices and profits will keep out competitors. These price cuts, in turn, will increase consumption, and the early oligopolists will retain a greater share of the increased market than if new competitors were to enter. A greater share of a larger market will enable the early oligopolists to build additional plants, thus gaining even more production experience. Moreover, these plants tend to be larger; hence, they provide lower costs. The low-price strategy might work best when the early oligopolists believe that their basic position, relative to that of potential competitors, is sufficiently good that price cuts will discourage others from entering. If prices are maintained at a high level, however, a "smart" potential entrant would realize that its entry would most likely cause prices to fall, so it would base its entry decision on the assumption of the lower prices. In cases in which the estimated lower price level still looks attractive to a potential entrant, it would be necessary for the existing producers to lower the price even further to keep out that entrant.

A firm adopting the low-price strategy assumes that later in the product's life, the growth rate in consumption will slow down, and potential newcomers will believe it difficult to overcome the low costs inherent in the accumulated production experience and large plants of the existing producers and decide not to enter the business. In those future years, so the argument goes, volume and price will be such that the discounted present value of projected future profits will be greater than the discounted value of the forgone profits that would have been available from the high-price strategy.

Since the number of competitors in most petrochemicals has increased gradually over time, often reaching a total of ten to fifteen in the United States and several dozen in the world, it seems likely that quite a few of the early oligopolists followed a strategy of keeping prices high and allowing other firms to enter. On the other hand, it is possible that they tried the low-price strategy, but subsequent entrants succeeded in innovating lower-cost processes. (Unfortunately, there is no way of knowing the proportion of entrants that had lower costs than the incumbents and the proportion that had costs identical to or higher than the incumbents.)

In either case, once the number of producers of a petrochemical reaches three or more and oligopoly control becomes difficult to maintain, the profit squeeze described in this chapter begins, and it lasts throughout the life of the product. To be sure, a major innovation will occasionally give one producer a decided advantage over others, and several producers may be forced to exit the business; but, before long, the forces of competition will again put the squeeze on profits of even that major innovator. Furthermore, even as some firms exit from the business and major process innovations become scarce, relief for existing producers does not necessarily follow. Even if there is a reduction in the number of competitors in one country, there can be increased competition from new producers abroad.

As chapter 6 illustrates, a key factor in the entry of additional competitors is the sale of technology.

CHAPTER 6

THE TRANSFER OF TECHNOLOGY

Petrochemical manufacturers almost invariably use in their own manufacturing facilities any commercially acceptable process they develop. Among the nine products, there are no exceptions to this practice. Manufacturers sometimes sell their technology to other manufacturers. In addition, engineering contractors obviously sell technology, since that is almost always their sole purpose for developing it. Besides developing their own processes, engineering contractors sometimes represent a petrochemical manufacturing company as the seller of the latter's technology. For example, the Badger Company, a U.S.-based engineering contractor, represents Standard Oil in the sale of its acrylonitrile process.

Willingness to transfer technology gives rise to the "manufacturing specialists" mentioned in chapter 4. These are firms that, despite the erosion of oligopoly profits, are able to compete by minimizing research and development and other overhead costs, and sometimes by selecting a narrow market niche in which to specialize. Among the nine products, an example of a company that has successfully adopted this strategy in the United States is Formosa Plastics Corporation U.S.A., a joint American-Taiwanese producer of vinyl chloride monomer. The company's executives hammer relentlessly on production costs. In 1981, they acquired from Imperial Chemical Industries, the British giant, a plant making vinyl chloride monomer in Baton Rouge, Louisiana. Within weeks, Formosa Plastics slashed personnel from 406 to 227, at the same time increasing output of the plant by 35 percent.[1]

Executives of large companies that spend considerable sums of money on R&D only to see their profits subsequently eroded by the entry of manufacturing specialists occasionally describe such companies in unflattering terms. For example, a disgruntled Du Pont executive, stung by the sharp decline in that firm's profits on synthetic fibers, was quoted in a *Business Week* interview about firms that did not develop their own technology. As he saw it, the excess manufacturing capacity that appeared in synthetic fibers during a recession was built "by companies who brought nothing but their greed to the game."[2]

Regardless of the frustration that some product and process innovators might feel, manufacturing specialists are an important part of the petrochemical industry, and the sale of technology to them represents an alternative source of profits for product and process innovators. In addition, technology is sold to other product and process innovators. The existence of manufacturing specialists and other firms willing to buy process technology makes companies with their own technology face two important questions: How does the technology owner decide whether to invest in a facility to use that technology or to sell the technology to an unrelated firm? If the decision is to invest, how does the technology owner decide whether the facility should be wholly owned or a joint venture with an unrelated firm? In the case of international transfers of technology, these questions are of importance to governments as well as to the enterprises involved in the transactions.

A priori, one would expect that if the market for arm's-length transfers does not work well, then intracompany transfers would dominate. Then, if, as the product gets older, the market works better because of more competitors, the share of arm's-length transfers should increase.

These and other issues that affect the channels used for the transfer of technology are explored below through an analysis of data for the nine products. The increase in the number of production facilities to make the nine products is illustrated in Figure 6-1. As of 1974, a total of 537 manufacturing units, each individually designed to make one of the nine products, had been built worldwide (excluding a relative few in the Centrally Planned Economies). Data were available for 515 of the plants. Because some of them used technology from more than one source, the 515 plants

Figure 6-1
Production Facilities Built during Specified Periods of Product's Life;
Average for Nine Products, Worldwide, through 1974

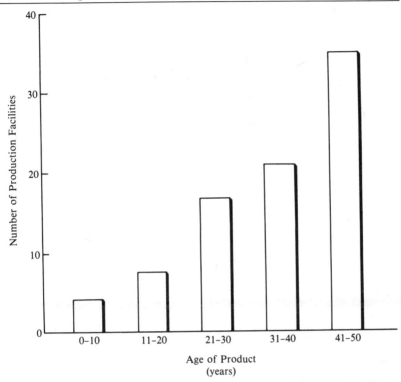

Note: The number of facilities existing each year between 1907 and 1974 was determined; facilities were then classified by age of product. Not all nine products are as old as 50 years, the span covered by this exhibit. The average number of the nine products that existed in each decade was 9 in the first and second; 8.5 in the third; 5.2 in the fourth; and 3.2 in the fifth. Thus, for example, an average of 8.5 products had entered the third decade of their life (age 21–30) as of 1974, and an average of 18 production facilities had been built during that decade of each product's life.
Source: Robert Stobaugh and Louis T. Wells, Jr., eds., *Technology Crossing Borders: The Choice, Transfer, and Management of International Technology* (Boston: Harvard Business School Press, 1984), p. 159.

involved 592 technology transfers, for 586 of which data could be had. By definition, a "technology transfer" occurred whenever a plant was built. In other words, the data include cases in which a company used its own technology as well as those in which a company sold technology to an unrelated firm. In addition to these two channels of transfer, a third involved investing in facilities jointly owned by the technology owner and another firm. Any given firm at any one time could employ all three channels simultaneously in different locations. The sale of technology to an unrelated party almost invariably involved granting a license allowing the purchaser to use the technology. This channel is referred to as "licensing." The term is not used to describe the transfer of technology to a facility owned, either wholly or partially, by the technology owner, even though sometimes such a transfer was also accompanied by a license.

Somewhat more than half of the 586 technology transfers were made by licensing to unrelated parties. In transfers that involved ownership, wholly owned subsidiaries heavily outnumbered the joint ventures, as shown in Figure 6-2.

LICENSING VERSUS INVESTING

The benefits and costs to the technology owner—hence the decision whether to license or invest—depend on a number of factors. As hypothesized above, a very important one is the competitive situation facing the technology-owning firm. Other factors are the size of the firm owning the technology, whether the transfer is international or domestic, and characteristics of the country in which the facility is to be located.[3] (The 139 transfers of technology by engineering contractors were excluded from this part of the study because, for strategic reasons, they do not normally invest in manufacturing facilities. Thus, the analysis includes only the 447 transfers by petrochemical manufacturers.)

The Importance of Competitors

There are several possible reasons for the influence of the number and type of competitors on the licensing-versus-investment decision. A manufacturing company that owns technology and uses it to manufacture a product can face competition in both the technology market and the product market. When there is only one owner of technology and one manufacturer, as was initially the

Figure 6-2
Transfers of Technology via Different Channels; Nine Products,
Worldwide, through 1974

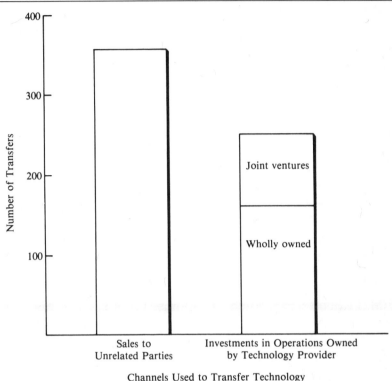

Channels Used to Transfer Technology

Source: Robert Stobaugh and Louis T. Wells, Jr., eds., *Technology Crossing Borders: The Choice, Transfer, and Management of International Technology* (Boston: Harvard Business School Press, 1984), p. 161.

case for each of the nine products, the return on investment is typically highest. Monopoly profits accrue to both the monopoly on technology and to the monopoly on manufacture. Therefore, product and process innovators are reluctant to sell technology early in the product's life, when there are few or no competitors. They fear, as chapter 5 showed, that an increase in the number of manufacturing competitors would reduce monopoly (or oligopoly) profits due to manufacturing. On the other hand, they are less reluctant to sell technology later in a product's life, when the existence of many competitors means that an innovator's market share is lower and oligopoly profits are slimmer.

One might suppose that an innovator could sell the technology for a price such that the competitor, because of its marginal cost, would prefer the product price that would maximize profits for the innovator. For example, a firm with a cost-saving technology would be able to sell it to competitors at a price that would leave the competitors' costs only marginally reduced. The process innovator would gain virtually all of the advantage from the innovation and leave virtually none of the advantage to a buyer. Under these conditions there would be no reason for a firm not to sell its technology.[4] In fact, there are a number of reasons why this technology-pricing practice does not seem to occur in the petrochemical industry.

A major impediment to this pricing practice is the substantial amount of uncertainty felt by both the buyer and seller as to exactly what the value of the technology will be to the purchaser.

First, the costs of the alternatives that might be open to the potential buyer are uncertain. The buyer, for example, might develop its own technology. Alternatively, in some cases the buyer could purchase technology from another firm (in which case, the costs would be known to the buyer but not to a competing potential seller). Even if another seller did not exist at the time, one could appear at any point in the future. The pricing decision facing the potential technology seller is somewhat similar to that facing the product seller, as discussed in chapter 5: that is, does the technology seller price the technology high and thereby encourage others to innovate a new process, or does the seller price it lower in order to discourage potential innovators?

A second reason for uncertainty is that sometimes the seller will not divulge all of its secrets before the sale. Because of the greater uncertainty, the potential buyer values the technology lower than the seller does.

Third, the seller needs to know the buyer's costs in order to know exactly what the technology is worth to the buyer. Some purchasers refuse to divulge such information, especially when an existing facility is to be modified to incorporate the new technology.[5]

Fourth, the value of the technology to the buyer depends on the volume of the buyer's output, which in itself is uncertain. Although the seller could attempt to cover this situation with a lump-sum payment for savings in fixed costs and an ongoing payment for savings in variable costs, the volume problem would still not be solved—in the long run, the volume affects the buyer's production costs by affecting its ability to lower costs through learning. The relation between cumulative production and lower costs is not so precise as to allow accurate prediction, because the lowering of costs depends on the efforts of the producing firm, themselves an uncertain factor.

Fifth, there is uncertainty involved in building and operating a new facility. In some cases, the uncertainty is even greater because the buyer is entering a new business. In either case, the appropriate return on the buyer's investment is an uncertainty.

In addition to uncertainty about the value of the technology to the potential purchaser, there are other factors that encourage firms to use their knowledge in their own facilities rather than to sell it to unrelated parties. First, technology owners fear a leak in proprietary knowledge. Licensees sign secrecy agreements, but the more people who know a secret, the greater the probability of a leak. Second, it is relatively easy for a technology owner, using its own technology in different markets, to maximize profits by charging higher product prices in some markets than in others. In contrast, prices for the technology cannot vary so widely. A firm selling its technology cannot reap the full benefit of high product prices that can be charged in some markets, unless, of course, there is a correspondence between producers and markets—a condition unlikely to exist over a long period. Even if this were the case, the "most favored company" clauses in licensing agreements tend to prevent the technology seller from price discriminating. Third, it is easier to set a price for the technology that will minimize total taxation by different national governments when the technology is used within the firm than when it is sold to an unrelated party.

To offset these factors, the technology purchaser must have an advantage over the seller in exploiting the technology. In international transfers, for example, such advantages might include knowledge of local conditions or government regulations as well as access to markets or to raw materials at a lower cost than might be available to a foreign firm. In this case, if there is only one seller and one potential buyer, as is sometimes the case in developing countries, the resulting bilateral concentration of power leads to an indeterminate or unstable bargaining situation when there is a range of prices satisfactory to both the seller and the buyer.

As competition in the technology and product markets increases, however, the impediments to technology transfers mentioned above become less significant. The result is a much greater tendency for the owner to be willing to sell the technology.[6]

As I have argued, considerable judgment is required in deciding whether to sell technology, and if the decision is to sell, how to price it. Discussions with industry executives and consultants about explicit cases as well as general rules of thumb suggest that technology sellers try to capture from 25 to 75 percent of the savings the purchaser will reap.[7] The exact amount depends on the seller's judgment of the factors described above, especially the alternatives open to potential buyers. The "most favored company" clauses also play an important role, since the initial sale has a major impact on prices that can be subsequently charged. And, of course, a subsequent sale can affect all previous sales if, as sometimes occurs, the contracts for these previous sales call for adjustments to royalty payments if subsequent contracts incorporated lower fees. The strong tendency to charge similar fees to all buyers means in itself that savings will differ among a heterogeneous group of buyers, because different buyers often have different unit costs for an identical input.

Examples follow that illustrate some of the factors involved in individual decisions. Dow refused to sell its technology (Dowlex) to make linear low-density polyethylene because it believed that its product was superior to that of all competitors. The company understandably did not want to sell a "crown jewel." Union Carbide, not possessing a technology to make a product with the same characteristics as Dow's product, did sell its technology (Unipol) to make linear low-density polyethylene; the price was sufficiently high to encourage the owner (British Petroleum) of a somewhat similar technology to sell its technology at a lower price than Union Carbide. When Du Pont was the only producer of nylon, it sold its technology to Chemstrand because it feared an antitrust suit.[8]

The analysis of the 447 transfers of technology for the nine products, on the part of petrochemical manufacturers, demonstrates the influence of competition, especially engineering contractors, on a manufacturing firm's decision to sell technology. Consistent with the a priori considerations mentioned earlier in this chapter, a company manufacturing a product with its own technology typically did not make its first sale of the technology until competition was well established. At the time of the first licensing for each of the nine products, the median number of other companies with alternative technology for making the product was eleven, ten of which used the technology in manufacturing. The initial sale occurred a median average of 22 years after the original commercialization, or about when engineering companies began to appear on the scene with their proprietary technology. In fact, for four of the nine products, engineering companies were the first to sell the technology.

Once the initial sale of technology for a product was made, licensing by manufacturing firms became widespread, accounting for 211 sales, as compared with 139 by engineering contractors. The greater the number of engineering contractors owning the technology, the higher the probability that a manufacturing firm would license rather than invest in its own facility. This was true for both domestic and international transfers. An increase in the number of manufacturing firms owning technology also increased the likelihood of a sale of technology in a domestic transfer by a manufacturing firm, but it did not seem to affect international transfers.[9] This suggests that increased competition by manufacturers has a greater impact on a firm in its home market than it does in its foreign market.

The Importance of Firm Size

As with product innovation, the size of a firm also plays an important role in determining its propensity to sell technology. Small manufacturing firms (with annual sales as the measurement of size) were much more likely to transfer technology through arm's-length sales rather than through investment in their own plants. There are several possible explanations for this pattern.

First, small firms are less able to bear the risk of the capital investment. This is an especially important consideration in petrochemicals, where economies of scale in manufacturing dictate that a relatively large—and costly—plant must be built in order for the firm to be economically competitive. Since greater risk is involved in investing abroad than at home, the size of the firm had even more influence on the international transfer decision than on the domestic transfer decision. Small firms were even more likely to opt for licensing rather than investing when an international transfer was involved.[10]

Second, the marginal costs of the additional management needed to operate a new facility, especially one located abroad, are likely to be higher for small firms. Since each new executive added to the payroll represents a commitment by the firm to pay salary, benefits, and expenses for a number of years, the addition of executives for a new facility is a larger consideration for a small firm than a big one. Furthermore, a big firm is more likely to have greater foreign experience, and so have in its employ one or more executives with the right experience.

Third, in the petrochemical industry, a small firm is likely to have a smaller market share in the product because small firms, like large ones, tend to diversify in a number of businesses in order to lower risk. Therefore, in some instances, the small firm would expect to incur a lower absolute cost in creating another manufacturing competitor than would a large firm. For example, a firm with a 10 percent market share probably would experience a lower absolute loss because of competition from a new entrant than would a firm with a 20 percent share. In some cases, however, the firm with the larger market share would be better able to withstand the additional competition because of the higher profit margins sometimes associated with larger market shares, which result in lower costs due to larger plants and greater experience.

Given these general considerations, it is not surprising that engineering contractors almost always license rather than invest. Typically they are smaller than manufacturing firms and have no experience in manufacturing petrochemicals—and thus no market share to protect.

International versus Domestic Technology Transfers

Seventy-six percent of the international transfers, but only 42 percent of the domestic transfers, involved licensing. Why does crossing a national boundary make a difference? Most petrochemical firms have less extensive operating experience in any single foreign country than in their home country. This translates into fewer resources—especially management skills and knowledge of local conditions—for foreign operations than for domestic operations. Managers also realize that there is greater risk in operating abroad than in one's own country. The risks range from misjudging the market to nationalization.[11]

Two other differences between international and domestic transfers affect the propensity to license at home compared with abroad.

The first difference is the possible effect on competition. Most petrochemical firms have larger sales for any given product in their home market than in any single foreign market. Thus, greater competition in the home market is likely to be more costly to them in terms of lower prices and lost sales than greater competition in a foreign market would be. And a licensee manufacturing domestically is apt to be more of a competitor in the technology seller's home market than would a licensee manufacturing abroad, because of tariff and freight charges and the insecurity of supply inherent in importing. As mentioned above, the analysis of the importance of competitors indicates that the level of competition in a firm's domestic market did affect its willingness to license more than did the level of competition in foreign markets. Still, the desire to protect the domestic market was not an overwhelming factor in every case. Of the initial sales of technology for each of the nine products, four were within the seller's home country.

Another difference between international and domestic transfers is that some nations receiving technology—Japan, Mexico, and India, for example—have required petrochemical plants to be locally owned and controlled.[12] Governments want to keep as much control as they can in the hands of nationals.[13] Although the desire of some technology-importing nations for local ownership is important in individual instances, it does not play an important role in explaining the worldwide pattern of transfers used for the nine products. There were simply too few instances of transfers to countries with a strong policy favoring local ownership to make a significant difference in the totals.

The Importance of Industrial Development and Large Markets

Two characteristics of the nation where the technology was to be used affected the licensing/investment decision: the stage of industrial development and the size of the market.[14] These two characteristics, of course, are often found in the same country: that is, most large-market countries are also highly developed ones.

The owners of technology showed a greater tendency to use licensing (rather than foreign direct investment) to transfer technology to developed countries than to less-developed ones. Firms capable of purchasing the technology and operating the facilities are more likely to be found in developed countries. One could argue, of course, that the local entity in a developing country needs nothing but money to purchase the technology, since the potential purchaser could hire someone to manage the project, operate the facility, and market the output. This pattern, however, has seldom been followed in the petrochemical industry; most firms purchasing technology have had at least some previous knowledge of the industry.

Mixed evidence was found concerning the impact of the size of the host country's market on the decision to license or invest. Managers of technology-owning firms stated in interviews that they prefer investment over licensing when the technology is to be used in a large-market country, for the simple reason that they want to use available managerial resources in countries with the greatest economic potential.[15] In contrast, the analysis of the 447 transfers showed that a company transferring technology into a large-market country was more likely to sell it to an unrelated firm than was the case in transfers to small-market nations.

There are several possible explanations for the discrepancy between what managers said and what they actually did. First, it could be a statistical artifact resulting from the fact, already pointed out, that most large-market countries are also highly developed ones. (There was a statistically significant correlation between these two variables.)

Second, licensing arrangements in large-market countries may have been part of reciprocal agreements under which firms grant licenses in order to be allowed to purchase technologies owned by other firms. Such reciprocal licensing can result either from formal agreements between firms or from informal understandings that reflect a live-and-let-live practice in the industry. It is most likely to occur between large firms, which are usually headquartered in large-market nations. There was no evidence, however, to support the notion that reciprocal licensing was widespread.[16]

A third possibility is that large markets may have been more competitive, therefore less attractive for investment. Though all these factors may have contributed to the inconsistency between managers' views of licensing in large-market countries and their actual behavior, the latter explanation—the existence of entrenched competitors—seems most compelling to me.

INVESTING: JOINT VENTURES VERSUS WHOLLY OWNED FACILITIES

The company that chooses to invest in a facility to utilize its technology faces a further important decision: should the investment be a joint venture with another firm, or should it be wholly owned by the investor? Some of the factors affecting the licensing/investment decision influenced this choice as well. Specifically, the propensity of a firm owning technology to enter into a joint venture was greater when a relatively small company was making the decision; when the transfer was an international one (in fact, joint ventures were seldom used for domestic investments); and when the technology was transferred to a developed, large-market country.[17]

The other key variable—the number of companies owning the technology—did not seem to affect the decision. Thus, in some respects, the degree of ownership seems to be an extension of the licensing/investment decision, as some of the factors that favor licensing over investment also favor joint ventures over wholly owned facilities.

CHANGING PATTERNS OVER TIME

The histories of the nine products support this chapter's earlier hypothesis that as the product gets older, the technology market gets more efficient, and arm's-length sales of technology increase. The histories, analyzed in chapters 2 and 4 as well as here, also suggest that patterns of technology transfer fall into three distinct phases (see Figure 6-3).

During the first period, which lasted for a decade or two for each product, the larger manufacturing firms in large-market, developed countries dominated the business. They developed their own technology and used it in facilities wholly owned by them and located in their home countries. The number of international technology transfers was virtually zero, and overall, the number of technology sales was very low.

During the second period, lasting another decade or two, the smaller manufacturing firms and engineering contractors began to develop their own technology. The smaller manufacturers employed their technology primarily in their own facilities, located in their home countries, while the engineering contractors sold their technology at home and abroad. The large manufacturing firms, in the meantime, began to invest abroad and to license at home and abroad. During this period, owners sold their technology about as often as they used it in their own facilities, with domestic transfers favoring investment and international ones favoring licensing. Of the transfers that involved investment by a technology-owning firm, some two-thirds of the international ones were joint ventures, whereas virtually none of the domestic ones were.

During the third period, which roughly corresponded to years thirty through fifty in a product's life, the number of transfers by large firms continued to increase, but was surpassed by the number of transfers by the smaller manufacturing firms and engineering contractors. The latter categories accounted for most technology transfers both at home and abroad. The engineering contractors, of course, concentrated on selling technology, whereas the smaller manufacturing firms sold technology and used it in their own facilities as well. In this period, some two-thirds of the transfers were international ones, and licensing became the dominant channel, accounting for almost 90 percent of the international

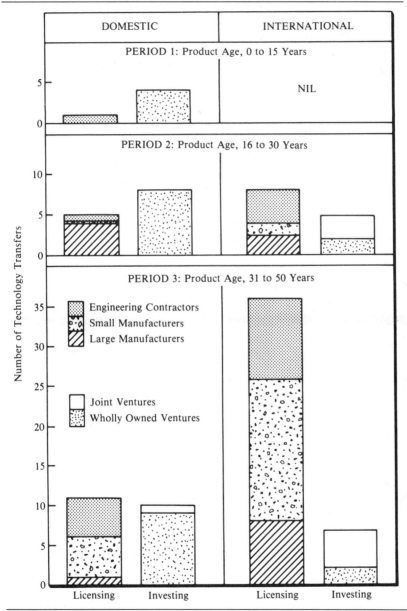

Figure 6-3

Channels for Transfer of Technology, during Three Time Periods in Products' Lives, Domestic Compared with International; Nine Products, Worldwide, through 1974

Source: Robert Stobaugh and Louis T. Wells, Jr., eds., *Technology Crossing Borders: The Choice, Transfer, and Management of International Technology* (Boston: Harvard Business School Press, 1984), p. 171.

transfers and slightly over half of the domestic ones. Of the transfers that involved investments by a technology owner, joint ventures continued to account for some two-thirds of the international transfers but for very few of the domestic ones.

These transfers of technology, especially the international ones, are accompanied by changes in international production and trade patterns.

CHAPTER 7

INTERNATIONAL PRODUCTION AND TRADE PATTERNS

There is a systematic pattern in which firms in different nations begin production of a given petrochemical product. The concept of a nation's "production imitation lag" is useful in explaining this pattern. A nation's production imitation lag for a given product is the amount of time between its first commercial production in the world and its first commercial production in the specified country. The manufacture of a product commences earlier in a country with a short production imitation lag than in a country with a long imitation lag.

The production imitation lags for the nine products are illustrated in Table 7-1, which shows a wide range of years from the date when each product was initially commercialized in either Germany or the United States, and the start-up of commercial production facilities in other nations around the world. The imitation lag between the first nation to commercialize a product and the second to do so was typically seven years, and another four years until a third country commenced production (medians from Table 7-1). Some countries began their first manufacture of the products some forty to fifty years after the initial commercialization. A striking feature of this worldwide pattern of production is the relatively long time lags.

One might suppose that petrochemicals have longer production imitation lags than certain other products because petrochemicals might move more easily through trade because of transport costs

Table 7-1
Production Imitation Lag of Countries Manufacturing Nine Products (Measured in Years after Initial Commercialization, as of 1974)

Product[a] Year of Initial Commercialization	VC 1927	MN 1923	SM 1931	PN 1907	CH 1942	AN 1933	OX 1945	PX 1949	IP 1944
Country[b]									
United States	2	3	4	7	0	7	0	0	0
EEC									
Germany[c]	0	0	0	0	28	0	18	13	
France	14	6	25	46	9	22	17	13	
Italy	13	11	20	51	21	23	18	15	27
Benelux	22	44	29	51	23	36	25	21	18
Japan	12	10	28	8	14	21	15	10	28
United Kingdom	13	5	22	27	7	26	17	6	
Canada	16	30	12	46	20	33			
Spain	23	39	42	38	28	39	22	22	
Mexico	40		36		25	38	19	25	
India	34	43	32	60			28	24	
Australia	22	20	30	35					
Sweden	18								
Argentina	33	42	34	52					
Switzerland	15								
Brazil	27	36	26	53	24				
Austria	26	38		53					
South Africa	27	38	33						

	VC	MN	SM	PN	CH	AN	OX	PX	IP
Finland	45	47							
Norway	23	43							
Pakistan		44							
Portugal	36								
Philippines	38								
Turkey	43	43	43						
Israel	37	50							
Colombia	39								
Greece	40								
Taiwan	30	43							
South Korea	40	48			39				
Peru	40			39					
Thailand	45								
Trinidad			21						

Key:
VC = vinyl chloride monomer
MN = synthetic methanol
SM = styrene monomer
PN = synthetic phenol
CH = cyclohexane
AN = acrylonitrile
OX = orthoxylene
PX = paraxylene
IP = isoprene

[a] Ranked by number of companies producing product in 1974, i.e., VC was made by more firms than MN, which, in turn, was made by more firms than SM, and so on.

[b] Ranked by market size as measured by manufacturing output in 1974. Without regard to the EEC, the countries would have ranked as follows: United States, West Germany, Japan, France, United Kingdom, Italy, Benelux, Canada, and so on as above. Between the earlier periods, when production was begun in a number of countries, and 1974, there were some changes in rank, but not a great deal. The major changes, for example, between 1958 and 1974, were the increase in rank by Japan and the decline by the United Kingdom.

[c] Germany prior to World War II; West Germany thereafter.

Sources: Industry trade journals plus author's questionnaire.

and/or less advantage for a local supplier. A comparison of electronics and petrochemicals, however, does not support this hypothesis. Compared with petrochemicals, semiconductors have lower transport costs and about the same advantages for a local supplier, yet manufacturing facilities for new semiconductors usually have been built abroad just a few years after the original commercialization.[1] Rather, several other factors seem to contribute to the longer production imitation lags in petrochemicals. First, as previous chapters have shown, the reluctance of the original product innovator to sell the technology forces any early would-be producers to develop their own technology. Second, unlike some instances in electronics, an existing petrochemical facility usually cannot be converted economically to make a different product. Thus, a new facility is needed; and it takes several years to design and build a petrochemical plant even if the plant is similar to ones already existing. And third, relatively long lead times are required for a market to be developed for a particular petrochemical product.

INTERNATIONAL PRODUCTION PATTERNS

Four variables appear to have been important in determining the pecking order of nations in commencing production of a given petrochemical product.[2] They are market size, availability of locally developed technology, investment climate, and shipping costs.

Market Size

Large markets were shown to be important in encouraging product innovation (chapter 4) and in affecting the sale of technology (chapter 6). Market size also helps determine the order in which nations begin the manufacture of petrochemicals. Indeed, the size of market is the most important factor affecting a country's production imitation lag. In previous chapters, large-market nations were defined as those with relatively high populations and incomes. In the present chapter, that definition is refined further to mean nations with relatively high manufacturing output. This term is used as a proxy for market size, because measuring consumption, either actual or potential, of a given petrochemical product can be difficult. For example, if the product is already being consumed in a country without a manufacturing facility, the amount and expected growth of imports serve as a guide to potential market size. But sometimes import statistics for individual petrochemicals are not available. Furthermore, consumption in a country may increase substantially once a manufacturing plant is located there.

In addition, since virtually all petrochemicals are used in the manufacture of other petrochemicals or end products made from petrochemicals, the *potential* consumption of a given petrochemical may be much larger than *actual* consumption because no manufacturing plant consuming the product has yet been erected in the market. For example, large quantities of synthetic rubber were used to make tires in Argentina, but styrene and butadiene—intermediates in the making of synthetic rubber—were not consumed in that country because there was no synthetic rubber manufacturing plant there. The situation changed, however, when a synthetic rubber plant was built, along with plants for styrene and butadiene—all in a single project.[3]

For these reasons, the total output of all types of manufacturers is a good proxy variable of a country's market size for petrochemicals in general. When market size is measured by manufacturing output, the data indicate that countries with small markets begin production of a given product later than countries with large markets. In other words, small-market countries have longer imitation lags. In the case of the nine products, a country whose total manufacturing output was double that of another country typically began production three to four years before the smaller country.[4]

Table 7-1, which ranks countries in which production had begun by 1974 in order of market size, confirms at a glance the overwhelming importance of market size. The larger-market countries manufactured more of the nine products than did the smaller-market countries and generally started production of any given product earlier. Significantly, in only one of the 127 cases shown in Table 7-1 (and in only one of the 537 plants in the entire survey), was a plant built in a country without a demand for the product: in Trinidad, cyclohexane was made from feedstock obtained from a refinery utilizing Trinidadian crude oil.

The existence of only one export-based plant among the nine products is evidence of the manufacturers' historical perception that building a petrochemical plant to serve only export markets is a high-risk venture. Indeed, U.S. petrochemical executives questioned on this matter said they had never built in the United States a plant with its economic justification dependent upon exports. They believed that the export market would dry up as more nations began production of the petrochemical in question.[5] This aversion to risk, coupled with the economic advantages of building big plants and operating them near capacity, means that petrochemical plants were located traditionally in large-market countries—at least through 1974.

Once a country's market approaches the size needed to support a profitable operation, a number of other forces may encourage a manufacturer to build a plant. For instance, most manufacturers believe that sales will be greater from having a local plant than from exporting to a country, because of greater customer confidence that a local manufacturer can deliver a product on time. Also, manufacturers often fear that a rival, local or foreign, might preempt the market by building a plant and thereby obtaining greater tariff protection—an especially important consideration in less-developed countries.

Availability of Local Technology

The availability of locally developed technology is the second most important factor in explaining a country's production imitation lag. A longer lag occurs if technology is imported from abroad, regardless of whether it is transferred through licensing or by a direct investment of the technology-owning firm. In the case of the nine products, those countries that used locally developed technology tended to begin production about ten years before countries that had to import the technology.[6]

The reasons are consistent with the concepts introduced in earlier chapters. A local company that has developed technology suitable to produce a given product is likely to perceive fewer risks in investing in a local facility than a foreign investor would. Moreover, the local company would not face the problems associated with buying and selling technology.

Investment Climate

A third factor that determines a country's production imitation lag is that country's investment climate. This climate consists principally of economic and political conditions such as inflation, currency stability in foreign exchange markets, and discrimination against foreign-owned firms or those in certain industries. Tariffs, another component of investment climate, almost surely affect a country's imitation lag; however, a statistical analysis of the nine products failed to identify this effect. Unlike many other industries that consider hourly wage rates an important part of the investment climate, the petrochemical industry uses relatively small amounts of labor; hence, labor cost is not an important consideration.

A country's investment climate also depends on expectations about possible changes in political and economic conditions. Since many of these conditions depend on political stability, a number of authors have studied "political risk," which is considered to exist when unanticipated political changes may affect the corporation.[7] In spite of extensive interest in the subject, political risk analysis—and therefore investment climate analysis—is still not fully developed. Even though half of U.S.-based multinational enterprises are reported to evaluate political risks when investing abroad, the approaches used remain unstructured and unsystematic. Especially lacking are conceptual models that assess specific impacts on a particular firm or investment—the crucial item of concern to managers.[8]

Analysis of political risk is usually associated with foreign investments, but a number of items of concern to foreign investors—tariff protection, for example—also concern indigenous investors. Foreign and indigenous investors would be likely to have similar views on tariff protection. On certain other items, such as discrimination against foreign investors, however, their views would diverge. In either case, it is difficult to relate a general measure of investment climate to the profitability of individual investments, whether foreign-owned or locally owned. Nevertheless, a general rating scale used by one U.S.-based petrochemical manufacturer proved significant in explaining when countries began production of the nine products. A country with a high rating began production about ten years before a country with a low rating.[9]

Shipping Costs

The farther an importing country is from another country capable of supplying its needs, the higher the freight costs in obtaining the product. Consequently, the desire to avoid higher shipping costs is a factor in encouraging the earlier start-up of petrochemical production in countries remote from major producing centers: that is, remote countries have shorter production imitation lags than countries located near other producing countries. When the major production centers were the United States and Western Europe, such remote countries as Argentina, South Africa, Australia, and Japan began production of the nine products four years earlier, on average, than would have been expected from an analysis of the other variables.

Not only are shipping costs a prominent factor in determining the production imitation lags of different countries, they are also important in determining the production imitation lags of different products for any given country: in other words, high comparative shipping costs for a product, in relation to its value, reduce that product's imitation lag. Shipping costs for the same distance differ among products because of special handling facilities, such as pressurized containers, required to ship some products. Shipping costs for the nine products from the United States to Japan, for example, ranged from 4 percent of the price of acrylonitrile to 40 percent of that of vinyl chloride. This is an important factor because a high delivery cost for a product makes it more likely that a plant built in any given consuming country would be competitive with a plant in another country originally supplying the product. For example, among the nine products, a product with a shipping cost equivalent to 30 percent of its value for a specified distance was manufactured in a given country about four years before a product with a shipping cost equivalent to 10 percent of its value for the same distance.[10]

INTERNATIONAL TRADE PATTERNS

At roughly the same stage in the life of a petrochemical that the erosion of oligopoly profits begins to clear the way for domestic and international technology transfers, international shipment of the product also begins. In the case of the nine products, the average lag between initial commercial production in the United States and initial U.S. exports was fourteen years.[11]

The reason for the pause that occurred between the initial commercialization and the first international shipments is that foreign markets were being served first by exports of final products—seat covers, carpets, clothes, for example—followed by exports of intermediate products such as plastic resins and fibers, rather than by exports of basic petrochemicals like the nine products.

Eventually, however, international shipments do begin, as manufacturers of these intermediate and final products spring up in foreign markets. Early exporters—like early producers—of a petrochemical are able to earn substantial profits. Early exporters can keep prices high in a foreign market because often there is little competition in that market. Thus, even after shipping costs and tariffs are subtracted, profit margins for an exporter in an oligopoly situation may be high. Increasing competition, however, stemming from process innovations and international technology transfers, then causes export profits to erode in a systematic pattern as the product moves through several distinct stages of international trade. This pattern is important not only to executives planning strategy, but also to government officials setting investment and trade policies.

Technology-Gap Shipments

Among the nine products, by the time international shipments of a product began, there were three or so countries in which production was taking place. Producers in those countries seldom shipped to one of the other countries that harbored a producer. Instead, they shipped to countries that had no production facilities. Shipments to nonproducing countries can be dubbed "technology-gap" shipments to denote the gap between the technology available in the exporting country and that available in the importing country.

Later, even after companies become willing to transfer the technology abroad, nations with a demand for the product still have to import it if their market is not large enough to encourage a company to build a plant. These shipments could be called "market-gap" shipments. However, because it would be difficult to distinguish market-gap shipments from technology-gap shipments, only one of the terms—technology-gap shipments—is used here to cover all exports of a petrochemical to a country that does not produce it.

Once undertaken, U.S. exports usually have grown at a faster rate than domestic consumption until the buildup in facilities abroad causes exports to taper off. This decline can be measured using exports as a percentage of domestic production. The upper part of Table 7-2 illustrates the progression for the three of the nine products that were originally commercialized in the United States and for which data were available.[12] In each of the three cases the export peak, or highest percentage, was far higher than the chemical-industry average of about 5 percent of U.S. production.[13] Gradually, however, exports as a percent of production moved down, from a peak average of 53 percent for the three products, to 22 percent in 1973.

Table 7-2 also illustrates the export advantage enjoyed by a country that harbors the initial producer of a petrochemical. Of the nine products, for the five that were originally produced in Germany, the U.S. export peak averaged only 19 percent of production, compared with 53 percent for the three that were commercialized in the United States. Moreover, the table shows that for these three products, the greater the number of years that elapsed after the United States started production and before any other country began, the higher the U.S. export peak. The difference in export performance stems from the temporary monopoly enjoyed by the initial producer. Furthermore, this advantage is sustained even after production has commenced abroad, because the early producer gains valuable experience that helps lower costs so it can compete effectively in world markets.

With the addition of producers abroad, the early producer inevitably loses some of its foreign markets. In addition, the new pro-

Table 7-2

U.S. Production Lead and Export Peak, Eight Petrochemicals, Year of Initial Commercialization through 1973[a]

Country of Initial Commercialization	Product	Production Lead of United States over Rest of World (years)	U.S. Exports as a Percentage of U.S. Production		
			Peak year	In peak year	In 1973
Products initially commercialized in United States:					
United States	Orthoxylene	15	1960	87%	34%
United States	Cyclohexane	7	1967	47	24
United States	Paraxylene	6	1965	25	7
	Average	9		53%	22%
Products not initially commercialized in United States:					
Germany	Acrylonitrile	−7[b]	1963	27%	8%
Germany	Synthetic phenol	−7	1943	16	5
Germany	Styrene monomer	−4	1969	18	10
Germany	Synthetic methanol	−3	1972	16	12
Germany	Vinyl chloride monomer	−2	1970	16	8
	Average	−5		19%	9%

[a] Export data for one of the nine products, isoprene, were not available.
[b] This means that the United States started production seven years after the initial commercializing nation: i.e., had a production imitation lag of seven years.
General note: The coefficient of correlation (r) between "Production Lead of United States" and "U.S. export peak as a percentage of U.S. production" for these eight products is significant at greater than 95 percent confidence level.
Sources: Production data from U.S. Tariff Commission, *Synthetic Organic Chemicals—U.S. Production and Sales* (Washington, DC: GPO), annual (*Trade* Commission in 1973 and thereafter). Export data from Bureau of the Census, *U.S. Exports of Domestic and Foreign Merchandise, FT-140* (Washington, DC: GPO, December issues), various years. These sources were supplemented by data from files of consulting firm and from chemical industry trade journals.

ducer also begins to cut into the early exporter's share of other foreign markets.

Balancing Shipments

When a country begins production of a petrochemical, it may cease to import the product, but often it must once again turn to foreign suppliers to meet domestic demand. Likewise, the country may have to stop exporting surplus product in order to meet domestic demand. The shift in trade pattern for a given petrochemical occurs because new capacity in petrochemicals can be added only in fairly large steps, while consumption rises gradu-

Figure 7-1
Idealized Relationship, Capacity and Consumption, One Product in a
Country Not the Original Commercializer

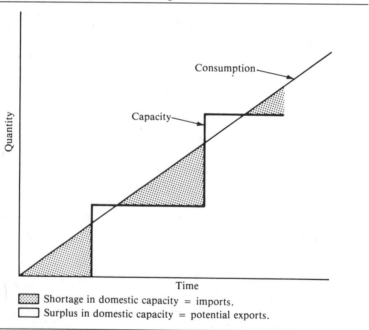

Shortage in domestic capacity = imports.
Surplus in domestic capacity = potential exports.

Source: Robert Stobaugh, "The Neotechnology Account of International Trade: The Case of Petrochemicals," *Journal of International Business,* Fall 1971, p. 54.

ally.[14] Thus, there is likely to be either a shortage or surplus of capacity in any given country at any given time.

Figure 7-1 shows the typical relationship between capacity and consumption for one product in a country that is not the original commercializer of the product. After the country has imported for a while, a company builds a plant and commences production (the first vertical step in Figure 7-1). Initially, there will be some excess product, which may be exported, but after a few years all available capacity is used to meet increased domestic demand. At this point, the country must begin to import once again in order to balance supply with demand—hence the term "balancing shipments." The term is used to denote all shipments to countries that produce the product. Later, when another plant or addition is built, the nation may have a surplus of product, which will be exported. Thus, a country vacillates between shortage and surplus of supply. Balancing shipments can be seen as a second stage in the pattern of international trade, with technology-gap shipments representing a first stage (see Figure 7-2).

Any country—even the initial producer—can need balancing shipments. The case of styrene monomer in Germany provides an example. Imports of styrene monomer into West Germany were negligible during the few years prior to 1964 and 1965 because the country had adequate capacity. In 1964 and 1965, however, imports from the United States were required to balance supply and demand. In 1966, these shipments dropped off sharply as a new styrene plant came onstream in West Germany.[15]

There are several situations other than a national shortage that can necessitate imports.

One theoretical model of international trade states that international oligopolists treat each national market as independent of others and behave so that each firm ships to each market.[16] This trade is called "reciprocal dumping," since the model specifies that the export prices would be below the domestic prices. A review of data for the nine products indicates that some reciprocal trade between countries does occur, although perhaps less extensively than suggested by the model; for in any given year, some countries with a domestic producer did not import product and some countries with a producer did not export. Furthermore, export prices to producing countries often were not lower than domestic prices in

Figure 7-2
Patterns of International Trade

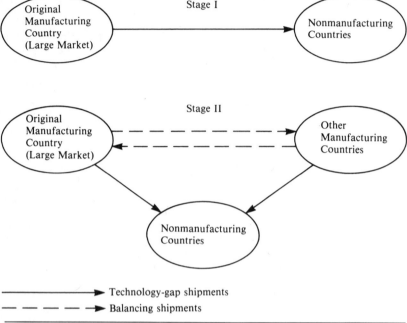

Stage I

Original Manufacturing Country (Large Market) → Nonmanufacturing Countries

Stage II

Original Manufacturing Country (Large Market) ⇄ Other Manufacturing Countries

Nonmanufacturing Countries

——————▶ Technology-gap shipments
— — — — —▶ Balancing shipments

the exporting country. Reciprocal trade, whether or not it involves dumping, often involves explicit recognition by an oligopolist of its competitors in other countries. For example, sometimes each of two firms located in different countries has exported a relatively small quantity of a product to the other country in order to achieve a competitive standoff. A French firm exporting to Germany would need to consider the reaction of a German firm exporting an identical product to France. The result is an implicit agreement for each firm to be the dominant producer and price setter in its home market and for neither firm to be very aggressive in competing in the other's market.[17]

In addition to such reciprocal trade, there are two other explanations of importation into a country that has no shortage. First, only one producer might exist in a country, but the local customers might desire several sources of supply. Second, a multinational firm might export to its subsidiary in a producing nation.

Both these situations are common in the petrochemical industry.[18]

Sometimes one or all of the three types of imports occur at the same time that the importing nation is exporting an identical commodity. Though not necessarily tied to a country's overall supply-and-demand situation, these kinds of imports also can be thought of as balancing shipments.

Once many countries commence production of a petrochemical, balancing shipments can become very important in relation to technology-gap shipments. During the late 1960s, exports to producing nations—or balancing shipments—accounted for three-fourths of U.S. exports of styrene monomer. In fact, for the nine products, balancing shipments from the United States increased from 12 percent of total U.S. exports of these petrochemicals during the early years of the products' lives to 62 percent of total U.S. exports during their later years.

Primarily because of balancing shipments, the absolute quantity of U.S. exports of the nine products typically did not decline, despite the continual addition of plants abroad. To be sure, in some years a shortage of the product in the United States resulted in a cutback in exports, since U.S. producers gave priority to their domestic customers. As soon as new plants were brought into production in the United States, exports resumed in substantial quantities. Exports of the nine products were still rising in absolute terms in the 1970s.

Managers of U.S. petrochemical companies have often failed to recognize the existence of balancing exports, and the failure has contributed to a belief that after reaching a peak, U.S. exports would decline to near zero and stay there. One typical statement referring to styrene in a 1959 trade journal said that most producers felt that 1959 would be the peak export year, after which overseas plants would cut sharply into exports.[19] In fact, though, the volume of U.S. exports of styrene monomer continued to rise and were twelve times as great in 1976 as in 1959. Some congressional testimony in 1968 indicated that the U.S. trade surplus in chemicals would decrease and reach zero by 1975 because of loss of export markets combined with increased imports resulting from the Kennedy Round of tariff agreements in the 1960s.[20] The U.S. trade surplus in chemicals continued to rise, however, and by 1976 it was more than twice as high as the 1968 level. Thus, the

Figure 7-3
Typical Patterns of U.S. Exports of a Petrochemical

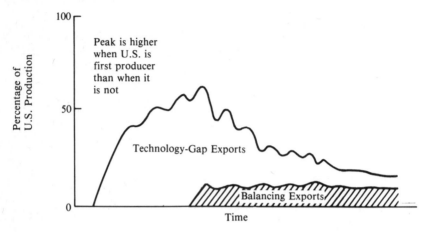

Relative To U.S. Production

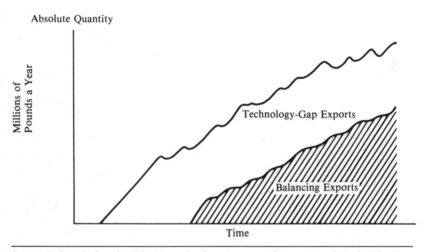

Absolute Quantity

Source: Robert Stobaugh, "The Neotechnology Account of International Trade: The Case of Petrochemicals," *Journal of International Business,* Fall 1971, p. 57.

existence of balancing exports can also have important implications for national policymakers.

Ignoring balancing exports has contributed to a shortage of petrochemical products in the United States and abroad. On a number of occasions, U.S. producers have rationed petrochemicals in both domestic and export markets—for example, styrene monomer in early 1973.[21]

Figure 7-3 illustrates the pattern of technology-gap shipments and balancing shipments, using U.S. exports as an example.

CHAPTER 8

THE CASE OF METHANOL

A closer look at the life of one of the nine products—methanol—illustrates the major points made thus far and introduces the concepts to be treated in the final chapters. Methanol is produced in many countries by a number of manufacturers. It is made from natural gas or naphtha and used to make fibers, plastics, and resins.

Methanol, like the other eight products and petrochemicals in general, was discovered by a scientist engaged in basic research rather than by a firm seeking profits. Robert Boyle, the British scientist famous for Boyle's Law, pertaining to the behavior of gases, is believed to have discovered methanol in 1661. In 1824, two French scientists, Jean-Baptiste Dumas and E. M. Péligot, were the first to establish methanol's identity.[1] In 1857, nearly two hundred years after Boyle's discovery, Berthelot first synthesized methanol from chemicals. From about this time, it was made commercially by the distillation of wood: hence, the name "wood alcohol."[2]

In 1921, Georges Patart applied for a patent in France for his process for making methanol from hydrogen and carbon monoxide. Patart's patent was published in 1922 and one year later Badische Anilin- & Soda-Fabrik (BASF) was the first company to produce synthetic methanol commercially, at Luena, Germany, using these raw materials and a high-pressure catalytic reaction process.

None of the nine products' innovators, including BASF in the case of synthetic methanol, held a patent on the product itself; instead, each patented the process for making it. Though BASF owned a number of patents in this area, it is not known whether BASF "borrowed" the process from Patart, refining it in the company's superior facilities, or developed it from independent research. It is known, however, that in 1913, BASF chemists had developed a synthetic methanol process that used a high-pressure catalytic reaction of carbon monoxide with hydrogen, and that commercial development of this process was delayed by World War I.[3]

Like the other eight products, synthetic methanol was commercialized in a large-market country—Germany, in this case, which had the world's second largest market. Also like the other products in this study, synthetic methanol was initially commercialized in the country where the product innovator had its headquarters. BASF was, and remains, a German firm with headquarters in Ludwigshafen am Rhein. Finally, the case of synthetic methanol is consistent with the finding that large firms are better suited than small firms for product innovation, since BASF was one of the giants of the chemical industry when it began producing synthetic methanol.

In the United States, the first imports of BASF's low-priced synthetic material in 1924 caused a turmoil, which led Du Pont to develop its own commercial process and open a plant in 1926. Thus, only three years after the initial commercialization of synthetic methanol, BASF's monopoly ended. It took only one year for Du Pont's manufacturing monopoly in the United States to come to an end, as Commercial Solvents developed its own process and opened a plant in 1927.[4] Firms that smell the aroma of another firm's monopoly are not easily shaken off!

Meanwhile, back in Germany, where synthetic methanol was originally commercialized, the second producer did not come along until 1947, much later than would be expected, given the commercial success of synthetic methanol in capturing virtually all of the methanol market from methanol produced via wood distillation. This delay, however, was caused by the cartelization of the German chemical industry from the mid-1920s until after World War II, which enabled one company to maintain its domestic monopoly for two decades.

In chapter 2, process innovations were categorized as major or minor. The difference between the two is that major innovations involve different raw materials or radically different reaction conditions. In the case of synthetic methanol, there were six major innovations and twenty-five minor innovations between the time of the initial commercialization and 1974. Consistent with the pattern demonstrated by the other eight products, the number of innovations, especially major ones, tended to decrease as the product matured (see Figure 8-1).

Although it is unusual, major innovations do occur for old petrochemicals. In 1966, forty-three years after synthetic methanol was commercialized, Imperial Chemical Industries (ICI) began producing synthetic methanol commercially with a new low-pressure process at a plant in Billingham, England.

As the cases of Alpha and Beta demonstrated in chapter 3, the development of a new petrochemical product or major innovation takes a long, difficult, and uncertain journey. The roots for ICI's

Figure 8-1
Number of New Processes Developed in Each Decade of Synthetic Methanol's Life, Original Commercialization through 1974

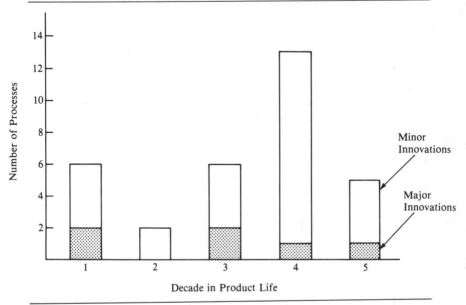

Sources: Industry trade journals and author's questionnaire.

low-pressure process began in the late 1950s, when work began to develop a process to reform naphtha in the presence of steam. In turn, this process, when commercially introduced in 1962, gave researchers sulfur-free synthesis gas, thereby allowing the development of a stable copper-type catalyst that met the commercial requirements for activity, selectivity, and longevity. It took almost five years of additional research at Billingham to develop the catalyst and put it to work in a synthetic methanol plant.[5]

The importance of the new catalyst was that it allowed methanol conversion to occur at a low pressure. Existing processes operated at about 300 atmospheres of pressure (about 4,400 pounds per square inch), while the ICI process used a conversion pressure of about 50 atmospheres. In addition, conventional processes ran at temperatures of 570°–750°F, while the low-pressure required only 480°F. These factors gave ICI's process tremendous cost advantages, which stemmed from higher efficiency, lower energy consumption, longer catalyst life, increased reliability, lower maintenance costs, and greater economies of scale from larger plants. The low-pressure plants also had initial capital costs that were about 5 percent lower than those of high-pressure plants. The total manufacturing costs, fixed and variable, were about 6 percent lower with the low-pressure process.[6]

Fortunately for ICI, its new process was so good that it was used not only in most new plants, but it also caused some existing plants to be shut down or converted to the new process. The first company, other than ICI, to use the low-pressure technology was Monsanto, at a 100-million-gallons-per-year plant at Texas City, TX, which came onstream in 1970. The ICI process was rapidly adopted throughout the world. Other early licensors included Taesung Lumber Industrial Corp. of South Korea and Georgia Pacific in the United States.[7]

Of the 20 plants that came onstream between 1970 and 1974 in countries other than those with centrally planned economies, 12 used ICI technology. In the United States, the ICI process was employed in 3 of the 6 plants built in this period. The new process also contributed to the closing of older plants, as 16 were shut worldwide. By the end of 1984, there were 62 synthetic methanol plants operating throughout the world, including those in Centrally Planned Economies, and 25 of these used low-pressure-process technology provided by ICI.[8]

Chapter 4 pointed out that, although firms of various sizes have participated in process innovation, large firms possess an advantage over smaller firms. This is certainly borne out by the case of ICI, which at the time of its breakthrough was one of the largest chemical companies in the world. Moreover, ICI was already a leading licensor of synthetic methanol process technology, as well as a major producer, with plants in the United Kingdom, Australia, and South Africa.[9]

In 1971, Lurgi Mineralöltechnik, a chemical engineering firm based in West Germany, introduced its own low-pressure process, which also used a copper-type catalyst. Later that same year, Lurgi signed a contract to supply the technology to Veba Chemie for a plant at Gelsenkirchen, West Germany. Lurgi's technology was not a major innovation because it was not radically different from ICI's; still, it was attractive enough to become the second leading route to methanol. At the end of 1984, 10 of the 62 plants on line around the world, including those in centrally planned economies, used Lurgi's process. Combined, the two low-pressure processes accounted for slightly over half of the world's capacity by the early 1980s. In the industrialized world the new processes were even more dominant. By 1982, 100 percent of U.S. capacity used a low-pressure process (see Table 8-1), while 87 percent of capacity in Western Europe and 68 percent in Japan were based on low-pressure processes.

Chapter 5 examined the forces that cause petrochemical product prices and profits to decline in a systematic pattern over time, and the history of synthetic methanol shows it to be consistent with that pattern.

Table 8-1
U.S. Synthetic Methanol Capacity Based
on Low-Pressure Processes (percentage)

1970	10
1974	34
1978	50
1980	70
1982	100

Source: "CEH Marketing Report, Methanol," *Chemical Economics Handbook* (Stanford, CA: SRI International, October 1983), pp. 674.5022, L–M.

Beginning in 1930—the earliest year for which data are available—synthetic methanol production increased steadily. Following World War II, production increased much more rapidly with the growth of housing and the resultant consumption of plywood, held together by adhesives made from methanol-derived urea-formaldehyde resins. Production also grew as processes were developed for making acetic acid and chloromethanes from methanol feedstock. These developments, and others, resulted in methanol's becoming a major "building block" petrochemical used to make many chemicals, plastics, and fibers.

Table 8-2 demonstrates how increasing production and the concurrent increase in output per manufacturer, which is highly correlated with output per plant, contributed to lower prices by lowering manufacturing costs. For example, in 1933, when the average production per manufacturer was 2.5 million gallons per year, methanol sold for 29 cents per gallon, or the equivalent of $1.16 in 1973 dollars. Ten years later, the average production per manufacturer had risen to 14 million gallons per year, and the price had fallen to 69 cents per gallon (in 1973 dollars). Twenty years after that, in 1963, average production was up to 32 million gallons per year, while the price had dropped to 32 cents per gallon (in 1973 dollars), and finally by 1973, average production had risen to 118 million gallons per year, and the price was down to 11 cents per gallon.

The increases in output per manufacturer and accumulated production experience were accompanied by technological change made possible by developments outside the industry, which further lowered costs. In the 1960s, for example, equipment manufacturers developed large centrifugal compressors, which led to the construction of much larger methanol plants as plants with reciprocating compressors were replaced. Unit manufacturing costs for an 80-million-gallons-per-year plant with centrifugal compressors were estimated to be about two-thirds those of a 25-million-gallon-per-year plant with reciprocating compressors.[10] Celanese used centrifugal compressors in its 75-million-gallons-per-year plant at Bishop, TX, placed onstream in 1966, and this construction was followed in 1968 with Borden's 80-million-gallons-per-year plant at Geismar, LA, and by plants placed onstream by Hercules in 1969 and Du Pont in 1970. The use of centrifugal compressors in huge single-train plants lowered methanol manufacturing costs by 5–6 cents per gallon and contributed to the decline in market prices that occurred in the late 1960s and early 1970s.[11]

Chapter 6 looked at the patterns of technology transfer, and chapter 7 at international production and trade patterns. As discussed below, the record for synthetic methanol is consistent with those of the other eight products taken as a whole.

Among the nine, synthetic methanol was one of four for which the first technology sale was made by an engineering company. The first manufacturing specialist for methanol in the United States was Union Carbide, which opened a plant in 1929 using technology supplied by Nitrogen Engineering, a New York process-engineering company.

In the 1960s, ICI sold its technology only two years after first using it at Billingham, presumably because methanol was already a mature product. And since it was not the original innovator, ICI did not have a monopoly or huge market share to protect. It did not, however, initially license its technology to firms in countries where it had plants. In contrast, Lurgi, an engineering contractor that did not manufacture methanol, and hence had no market share to protect, licensed its first customer in Lurgi's home country, West Germany.

The lag between the first commercial production in Germany and exports to the United States was one year, while the production imitation lag was three years. All the early producers built plants in their home countries, each of which was a large-market country—a result consistent with the conclusion that market size is the most important factor in determining the pecking order of nations as manufacturers. Thus, it is not surprising that the eight plants constructed in the years between BASF's commercialization and World War II were located in the United States, England, France, Japan, and Italy.

Industry executives and many observers of the petrochemical universe, unaware of the changing pattern of balancing exports, have often expressed the opinion that U.S. exports of petrochemicals would taper off and eventually disappear. In the case of methanol, for example, it was widely believed at the beginning of the 1960s that U.S. exports would drop sharply by the middle of the

Table 8-2
U.S. Production and Sales of Synthetic Methanol

Year	Number of Producers[a]	Production (millions of gallons annually)	Average Production per Manufacturer. (millions of gallons annually)	Price[b] (cents per gallon)
1926	1	NA	NA	NA
1927	2	NA	NA	NA
1928	2	NA	NA	NA
1929	4	NA	NA	NA
1930	4	11	2.8	NA
1931	4	8	2.0	NA
1932	4	9	2.3	NA
1933	4	10	2.5	29
1934	4	16	4.0	32
1935	4	22	5.5	28
1936	4	30	7.5	28
1937	4	36	9.0	25
1938	4	29	7.3	26
1939	4	38	9.5	23
1940	4	49	12	22
1941	4	60	15	26
1942	4	67	17	26
1943	5	69	14	25
1944	5	75	15	24
1945	5	77	15	22
1946	5	79	16	21
1947	6	86	14	22
1948	7	152	22	25
1949	7	129	18	22
1950	7	138	20	22
1951	7	187	27	28
1952	7	168	24	27
1953	7	170	24	27

Table 8-2 Continued

Year	Number of Producers[a]	Production (millions of gallons annually)	Average Production per Manufacturer (millions of gallons annually)	Price[b] (cents per gallon)
1954	7	171	24	24
1955	8	205	26	25
1956	8	242	30	26
1957	8	231	29	26
1958	9	216	24	24
1959	9	267	30	19
1960	9	299	33	24
1961	9	309	34	24
1962	11	337	31	22
1963	11	353	32	22
1964	11	394	36	19
1965	11	433	39	20
1966	15	493	33	21
1967	14	520	37	20
1968	12	576	48	17
1969	12	634	53	18
1970	12	744	62	19
1971	11	747	68	13
1972	11	976	89	9
1973	9	1,065	118	11

NA = Sufficient data not published by U.S. government to enable the author to estimate figure; author unable to obtain such data from nongovernment sources.

[a] Includes some companies that produced methanol as a co-product and, therefore, might not appear on other lists of major methanol producers.

[b] Price calculated by dividing sales value by sales quantity. Statements in U.S. Tariff Commission *Information Series* indicate that the U.S. price during 1926–1929 approximated 66¢ per gallon.

Sources: Data for 1930–1965 from U.S. government sources presented in Stanford Research Institute, *Chemical Economics Handbook* (Stanford: SRI, 1966). Data for 1966 to 1973 from U.S. International Trade Commission, *Synthetic Organic Chemicals: U.S. Production and Sales* (Washington, DC: GPO), annual (*Tariff* Commission prior to 1973 report). Data for 1926 to 1929 from U.S. Tariff Commission, *Information Series* (Washington, DC: GPO), annual.

Table 8-3
U.S. Exports of Methanol

Year	Millions of Gallons Annually	Percentage of U.S. Production[a]
1930	1	8
1931	1	7
1932	1	8
1933	1	10
1934	1	5
1935	1	3
1936	1	2
1937	1	2
1938	neg.[b]	1
1939	1	3
1940	2	4
1941	neg.	1
1942	4	6
1943	2	2
1944	2	3
1945	2	2
1946	neg.	1
1947	neg.	neg.
1948	1	neg.
1949	1	neg.
1950	1	1
1951	1	1
1952	2	1
1953	3	2
1954	8	4
1955	6	3
1956	4	1
1957	6	2
1958	16	7

Table 8-3 Continued

Year	Millions of Gallons Annually	Percentage of U.S. Production[a]
1959	17	6
1960	30	10
1961	28	9
1962	22	6
1963	16	4
1964	56	14
1965	30	7
1966	8	2
1967	11	2
1968	11	2
1969	16	2
1970	44	6
1971	87	12
1972	163	17
1973	124	12

[a] Calculated from unrounded numbers.
[b] Neg. = less than 0.5.
Sources: 1930–1965 data from U.S. government sources presented in Stanford Research Institute, *Chemical Economics Handbook* (Stanford: Stanford Research Institute, 1966). Data for 1966 to 1973 production from U.S. International Trade Commission, *Synthetic Organic Chemicals: U.S. Production and Sales* (Washington, DC: GPO), annual (*Tariff* Commission prior to 1973 report). Export data for 1966 to 1973 from U.S. Bureau of the Census, *U.S. Exports: Schedule B Commodity by Country*, FT410 (Washington, DC: GPO), December issues of various years.

decade as a result of foreign capacity coming onstream and mounting tariffs. In 1961, for example, industry executives predicted that by 1965 exports would probably plummet to about 7 million gallons per year.[12] In fact, U.S. exports of methanol were 30 million gallons in 1965. Approximately 8 million gallons went to countries that did not manufacture methanol; 22 million gallons went to countries that did manufacture it. The result, as indicated in a 1965 trade journal: "Methanol is now in critically short supply. Producers have de-bottlenecked plants and made incremental expansion, but still export business has to be turned down and domestic buyers are on allocation."[13] True, exports did plummet in 1966 and stayed relatively low for a few years as the United States continued to be short of capacity. In the following years, however, exports grew spectacularly, and in 1972 they totaled six times those of 1961, when the dire prediction was made.

Since synthetic methanol was not commercialized originally in the United States, its highest export level relative to domestic production was only 17 percent, or considerably lower than the 53 percent average peak for products that were first produced in the United States (see Table 8-3).

PART II

After the 1973 Oil Crisis

CHAPTER 9

THE GOLDEN ERA ENDS

The period prior to 1973 may be described as the golden era of the industry. The oil shocks of 1973 and 1979 brought this period to an end, creating conditions never before experienced by the industry.

To portray the transition from a period of seemingly endless beneficence to one of continued disturbance, I compare in this chapter the dozen years before and subsequent to 1973. My focus is on the entire industry, but in some instances I use the nine products as examples because they are representative of the industry as a whole.[1] In other instances, data for the nine products are presented in various Notes.

THE GOLDEN ERA

The golden era was marked by rapid growth in markets, technological innovation, the appearance of giant plants, and a rush of new entrants into the industry. As a result of these developments, massive price declines occurred which amounted to 51 percent for the nine products in the dozen years before 1973.[2] Consumers as well as producers benefited. Lower prices and new products encouraged consumers to expand their purchases of petrochemicals. Between 1961 and 1973, there was an average yearly increase of 10 percent in U.S. petrochemical consumption, while markets abroad grew even faster.[3] The enlargement of markets enabled producers to increase their sales and profits in spite of lower prices. These favorable conditions generated a spirit of optimism, leading to the belief that there would be no end to the industry's golden era. The first oil shock revealed the shaky foundation on which this belief was based.

THE POST-GOLDEN ERA

These years can be divided into four periods.

The First Oil Shock, 1973–1975

The higher oil prices resulting from the cutback in oil production by Arab producers in 1973 meant higher costs for raw materials and energy for all petrochemical manufacturers. Therefore, petrochemical prices rose sharply. In the United States, for example, in spite of the moderating effect of price controls on U.S. oil and natural gas, petrochemical prices almost doubled between 1973 and 1975 (see Figure 9-1).[4] These price increases and the concurrent recession and inventory liquidation caused a decline in U.S. petrochemical production—about 20 percent during this period (see Figure 9-2).[5]

The drop in output, combined with the capacity expansions underway in 1973, intensified competition, causing profit margins to fall to a point at which the revenues received by a number of producers were not meeting the short-term cash costs involved in making and selling certain petrochemicals. The losses resulted in the shutdown of the less efficient facilities and the exit of a number of established producers from individual product lines. Between 1973 and the mid-to-late 1970s, for example, the average number of U.S. producers of the nine products dropped by 18 percent, in stark contrast to the 1961–1973 period, when the number rose an average of 71 percent.

Figure 9-1

U.S. Price Index for All U.S. Petrochemical Products, Compared with
U.S. GNP Price Deflator, 1973–1985

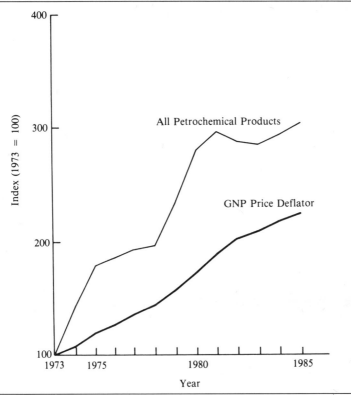

Sources: U.S. Department of Commerce, *U.S. Industrial Outlook* (Washington, DC: GPO),
1986, p. 11-2 and 1987, p. 11-4.

Optimism Revived, 1976–1979

Two factors played major roles in helping the petrochemical industry into a sharp recovery in the late 1970s. First, the world
economy rebounded strongly after its 1975 low. Second, higher
petrochemical prices had not, for the most part, made materials
derived from petrochemicals uncompetitive with metals, glass,
wood, natural fibers, and other materials, as many had feared.[6]

Figure 9-2
U.S. Production Index, Petrochemical Industry, Compared with U.S.
GNP Index, 1973–1985

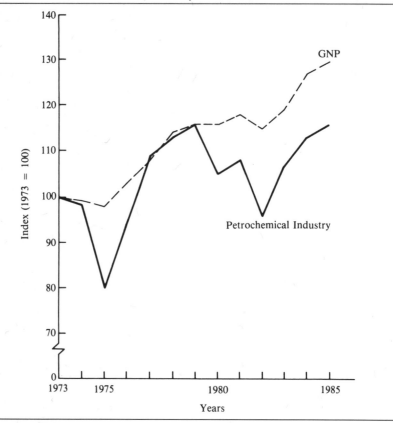

Note: GNP is in constant dollars.
Sources: U.S. Department of Commerce, *U.S. Industrial Outlook* (Washington, DC: GPO),
1986, p. 11-2 and 1987, p. 11-4.

U.S. production of petrochemicals bounced back, reaching new peaks in 1977, 1978, and 1979. In 1979, the U.S. production of petrochemicals was 45 percent above the 1975 level.[7]

By and large, industry executives, thinking this growth represented a resumption of the previous long-term growth patterns, began to add new capacity in large amounts. The businesses once more began to attract new entrants—some newcomers plus others restarting shutdown facilities. For example, for the nine products, between the low in the number of U.S. producers reached in the mid-to-late 1970s and a subsequent peak during the late 1970s and early 1980s, the number of U.S. producers increased by an average of 39 percent. A result of this movement was that industry executives, who for most of this period obviously were unaware of the forthcoming 1979 oil shock, again overbuilt their plant capacity. For example, U.S. consumption of methanol was up by 35 percent in 1976 over 1975, and an industry executive predicted that methanol consumption would increase by 8 to 10 percent per year. In fact, it grew by only 1 percent a year for the next two years and averaged only 4 percent a year from 1976 through 1985. The U.S. operating rate for methanol dropped from 93 percent in 1979 to 75 percent in 1980, as capacity was increased by 17 percent just when U.S. consumption dropped by 7 percent and U.S. exports dropped by 13 percent.[8]

Despair, 1980–1982

The 1979 jump in the price of crude oil shattered the price tranquillity that had existed in the oil market between 1975 and 1978. The hike in oil prices again caused prices of petrochemicals to rise sharply—some 50 percent in the United States between 1978 and 1981.[9] Higher petrochemical prices and the concurrent recession once again brought a downturn in the market for petrochemicals. Still, as late as 1981, a leading investment banking house was predicting a "very good" outlook for petrochemicals, including a bright 1982.[10] Instead, output hit bottom in 1982. From the peak year of 1979 to the 1982 low, the decline in output of the U.S. petrochemical industry was 17 percent.[11]

Massive additions of new capacity came onstream just as the second oil shock was causing this drop in petrochemical consumption. The result was vast overcapacity in the United States, Europe, and Japan. U.S. operating rates, for example, which had averaged 86 percent during the ten years ending in 1981, dropped as low as 65 percent in 1982. Profits of major U.S. petrochemical manufacturers fell to a 5 percent after-tax return on invested capital—about half their 1973 level. Elsewhere, the picture was even darker. In 1982, the major chemical companies headquartered in

Western Europe earned less than 1 percent on invested capital, and the major oil companies, headquartered in the United States and Europe, lost money on their chemical operations. All major petrochemical manufacturers experienced losses on some of their operations, with the damages running into billions of dollars. In Western Europe alone, estimates of losses in the year 1981–1982 ranged from $5 billion to $7 billion.[12]

This depressing situation caused a number of companies to shut down small, less efficient plants at a much faster rate than usual. It was "the long morning-after," as *Forbes* magazine called it.[13] In some cases, the companies quit certain markets by closing down foreign plants; in other cases, companies dropped the entire product line. The less efficient plants were shut down because revenues did not exceed the out-of-pocket expenses required to operate the business. In fact, profit margins were slim even for the firms with more efficient facilities; in most products, producers were struggling to achieve a positive margin of revenue over costs rather than an acceptable return on investment.[14]

For the nine products, for example, the average decline in the number of U.S. producers was 26 percent, compared with 18 percent in the 1973–1975 period. Usually, the producers with the smallest output were the ones that shut down their plants and exited from businesses, for their facilities were the smallest and least efficient. On the average, in the United States the plants that were shut down had about one-half the capacity of those that continued to operate.[15] The fact that the small plants were often the older plants and, in some cases, had considerably more cumulated production than the larger, newer ones indicates that the lower costs associated with larger plant size, and, in some cases, better technology, more than offset the lower costs that resulted from learning within the firm.

Some firms, especially in Europe and Japan, managed to reduce still further the number of competitors by merging a product business with that of a competitor or by swapping one business for another owned by a competitor. For example, mergers were extensive in Japan. In Europe, British Petroleum, which was strong in low-density polyethylene (LDPE) and weak in polyvinyl chloride (PVC), swapped its PVC business for ICI's LDPE business (ICI had been strong in PVC and weak in LDPE). After BP and ICI merged their newly acquired weaklings into strong businesses, they then reduced costs by closing their least efficient plants and cutting overlapping overhead costs in marketing, sales, R&D, and accounting. Still, the rationalization in Western Europe proceeded more slowly than if normal market forces had been allowed to operate; a combination of actions by some individual European countries and the EEC Commission kept some inefficient capacity in service and unduly delayed mergers and swaps among individual firms. Professor Joseph Bower of the Harvard Business School, in his study of the restructuring of the petrochemical industries in the industrialized nations, concluded that ". . . the rationalization of industry is most easily carried out by well-managed private companies," as occurred in the United States.[16]

One statement provides the flavor of what happened. Paul Oreffice, Dow Chemical's chief executive officer, quoted Dickens, saying that the early 1980s would be viewed as "the worst of times, the best of times": the worst of times for obvious reasons and the best of times because the industry moved away "from its mad capacity race and into a mode where everyone is trying to specialize more and do what they know best."[17] In spite of closures, mergers, and exchanges, the fundamental situation of the industry did not change—the major chemical companies were still highly diversified, and most petrochemical businesses still had many participants.

Modest Improvement, 1983–1985

During this period, modest declines in crude oil prices and a moderation in increases in both natural gas prices and general inflation were the major factors that caused a slight decline in the prices of petrochemicals. The price declines, along with the revival of the world economy, caused an increase in petrochemical output above the low of 1982—about 21 percent in the United States.[18] This market strength, combined with the reduction in the number of competitors, made it easier for firms to improve their profit margins from the very depressed levels of the 1981–1983 period. This time, however, the improvement did not cause a rush of new entrants—in the United States or elsewhere. In fact, in 1985, the number of producers in the United States was as low as in any year since 1973 for seven of the nine products.

Several factors contributed to the reluctance to enter, or re-enter, petrochemical businesses. For one thing, profit margins did not justify the construction of new facilities and manufacturers were unwilling to recommission and start up facilities they had shut down. Moreover, in spite of the growth in output from the 1982 low, the high levels of petrochemical prices had prevented the output of the industry from keeping up with the growth in GNP from 1973 to 1985 (see Figure 9-2). At the 1985 price levels, for example, the average prices (corrected for inflation) of the nine products were over *five times* as high as they would have been had the 1961–1973 price trends continued through 1985.

Unanswered was the question of how much of the slowdown in the growth of petrochemicals was due to a general maturation of the markets for the end products and how much was due to high prices. The high prices not only reduced the growth in the markets but also reduced the substitution of petrochemical end products for natural materials and reduced petrochemical usage in end products through conservation measures, such as thinner films and bottles, reduced solvent levels in coatings, and the substitution of foam for solid plastics. There was evidence, however, that the second oil shock had affected the competitive position of plastic materials vis-à-vis the other materials more negatively than the first had.[19]

OVERALL DEVELOPMENTS

Certain developments during the period 1973–1985 cannot be neatly classified into any one of the time segments discussed above, because they overlap several, or in some cases, all four periods.

Innovation

Economic theory suggests two reasons why innovation in the petrochemical industry should have decreased during the 1973–1985 period. The lack of expanding markets meant less opportunity to use new technology and the erratic nature of the markets meant higher risk in the development of new technology. Furthermore, as the patterns outlined in chapter 2 suggest, the rate of major innovation declines as a product ages, and beyond a certain point, the rate of minor innovations begins to decline as well. On the other hand, economic theory suggests that a dramatic boost in oil and gas prices should cause a surge in process innovation in order to make more efficient the use of raw materials and process energy.[20] Economic theory, therefore, is indeterminate in predicting whether innovation should have risen or fallen during the 1973–1985 period.

In fact, in petrochemicals, it is clear that there was a substantial slowdown in both product and process innovation after 1973. One study lists nine petrochemical product innovations of commercial significance during the 1960s and a mere two in the 1970s. Another study confirmed the findings, naming nine important product innovations between 1961 and 1973 and only two between 1973 and 1982 (the last year of the study). This same study listed ten important process innovations during the earlier period and three in the later period. Moreover, two of the three in the second period were commercialized shortly after the first oil crisis; thus, they had been underway before 1973.[21]

This trend affected the innovation of new processes to make the nine products. In the dozen years prior to 1973, the total for the nine products was 6 new processes that were classified as major innovations and 63 that were classified as minor innovations. In contrast, during the dozen years after 1973, 2 new processes were classified as major process innovations and 9 as minor innovations.[22]

Higher energy costs, however, did have some impact on the nature and rate of adoption of process innovation. In the case of methanol, for example, the low-pressure processes are much more energy-efficient than the high-pressure processes. Of the two new processes developed after 1973, both were low-pressure, energy-efficient processes. In 1973, about one-third of U.S. capacity used a low-pressure process. By 1982, all of it did. Six of the high-pressure plants existing in 1973 were converted to low-pressure operations and six other high-pressure plants were shut down.[23]

Transfer of Technology

On the international scene, the technology transfer patterns discussed in chapter 6 were maintained in the post-1973 years. All nine products were either in period 3 of the product life cycle (as shown in Figure 6-3) in 1974 or entered it a few years later. As would have been expected by this stage in the products' lives, licensing rather than direct investment by a technology innovator accounted for most (more than 80 percent) of the technology transfers.[24]

As it was for the nine products, process technology for most commercially important petrochemicals was readily available for purchase during the years 1973 to 1985. Faced with the possibility that other firms might develop competing technology for sale, even the developers of some new technologies that offered substantial improvements over existing technologies were willing to sell them.[25] The fact that some technologies were readily available for purchase allowed the continued construction of petrochemical facilities in countries that had not previously been producers.

International Production and Trade Patterns

Many of the newly producing countries were those in which a market existed for the product, a pattern quite consistent with that discussed in chapter 7. In a radical departure from this historical pattern, however, some plants began to be constructed in countries that were rich in oil and gas but that had no markets for the output of the facilities. As stated in chapter 7, only one of the 537 plants built worldwide through 1974 to manufacture one of the nine products was made in a country without a market for the plant's output. Between 1974 and 1985, though, 18 new plants to manufacture one of the nine products were built in countries rich in raw materials but without local markets of appreciable size. The appearance of these natural-resource-dependent, export-based plants is an important new trend, but 18 is a relatively small number of new plants compared with the 192 new ones built to manufacture one of the nine products in the non-communist world during this period.

Shipping costs and the complexity of production processes are two important factors affecting the attractiveness of building plants in hydrocarbon-rich countries to serve the export market. The cost of shipping the raw material from which a product is made is important, because this cost sets a floor price on the alternative value of the raw material in the export market. A high shipping cost results in a very low local value for the raw material. The complexity of the production process used to make the product is also important because, typically, new plants cost more in the small-market, hydrocarbon-rich countries because of lack of infrastructure in such countries. There is, therefore, a trade-off between the potential raw-material savings and the cost of the facilities. Hydrocarbon-rich countries with small domestic markets have their greatest cost advantage in products that can be made in simple plants with methane as a raw material. Methane is the most expensive of the hydrocarbon raw materials to ship because it must be transported at a very low temperature. It is, of course, a major constituent in natural gas, often accounting for 80 to 95 percent of the content.

Given this situation, it is not surprising that synthetic methanol is the only one of the nine products for which a large number of plants have been built in hydrocarbon-rich countries to serve the export market. It is the only one of the nine that can be made solely from methane. Furthermore, the manufacturing process starts with methane and produces methanol without the necessity of making intermediate products. The attraction of a methanol facility to a gas-rich country with a small methanol market is that there is also likely to be a small local market for natural gas, which means that natural gas has a low value in any alternative use. In some cases, the only alternative use of the gas is to leave it in the ground. In other cases in which gas is co-produced with oil, the alternatives are to compress and re-inject it to increase eventual oil output, or when this is not economic, to burn it as waste.

Of the 18 export-dependent plants built in the 1974–1985 period to manufacture one of the nine products, 14 were methanol plants, or about half of the 27 methanol plants built in non-communist countries during this period. All 14 plants were large-scale, used natural gas as raw material, and were based on purchased technology. Surprisingly, only 5 were in OPEC nations—Algeria (1), Libya (2), and Saudi Arabia (2). The remaining 9 were in Bahrain (1), Canada (4), Malaysia (1), New Zealand (2), and Trinidad (1). With the exception of Canada, none of these non-OPEC countries was a large oil producer, and none had enormous deposits of natural gas. Thus, only modest reserves of natural gas in excess of those required to fuel the home market were needed in order to have an adequate supply to feed a methanol plant.[26]

As a result of the buildup of export-dependent plants, the share of the world production capacity of methanol built to serve the export market increased from 9 percent in 1981 to 45 percent in 1985. This led to large-scale shutdowns of production capacity in the United States and other major industrial countries. For example, Japanese capacity was reduced by 50 percent in 1982, and U.S. capacity by 23 percent in 1985.[27]

After methane, the next most expensive hydrocarbon raw materials to ship are ethane and propane. These materials, like methane, are found in natural gas, and must also be shipped under pressure and/or at low temperature. Thus, the two of the other nine products (acrylonitrile and vinyl chloride monomer) that use methane and either ethane or propane as raw materials would appear to be likely candidates for manufacture in small-market, hydrocarbon-rich countries. Acrylonitrile is made from ammonia and propylene, which in turn can be made from methane and propane, respectively. The necessity of first producing ammonia and propylene for conversion to acrylonitrile, however, renders the overall process relatively complicated and costly. Therefore, manufacturing acrylonitrile is not such a clear economic winner for a gas-rich country as is producing methanol from methane. A similar but less strong rationale holds for vinyl chloride monomer, which is also relatively complicated and costly to manufacture, starting with the basic raw materials and energy source—salt, ethane, and natural gas.[28] In fact, several export-oriented vinyl chloride monomer plants have recently been built—in Alberta and Saudi Arabia.

In addition to methanol, two other major petrochemical products have also been attractive for hydrocarbon-rich countries with small markets—ammonia and ethylene. Ammonia can be made directly from methane without intermediate products, while ethylene can be made directly from ethane. Ammonia can readily be shipped or converted into urea, which has even lower shipping costs. Well over a dozen ammonia and urea plants have been built in hydrocarbon-rich countries. Since ammonia and urea are fetilizers, and worldwide demand for fertilizers was growing rapidly, these products entered international commerce with a minimum of fuss, although there were complaints from U.S. ammonia producers.[29] Ethylene, which is a gas at atmospheric temperatures, is also quite costly to ship. Thus, hydrocarbon-rich countries interested in building ethylene plants must also build downstream plants that use ethylene to make such products as polyethylene, ethylene oxide, ethanol, styrene monomer, and vinyl chloride monomer. Beginning in the mid-1970s, a number of world-scale, export-dependent, ethylene-based complexes were planned for hydrocarbon-rich countries. Many died in the planning stage as these countries came under increasing financial pressure when oil prices started to fall in 1981. The major success story in terms of completing a major export-oriented petrochemical complex, including ethylene and its derivatives, was that of Saudi Arabia.[30]

The Case of Saudi Arabia. Saudi Arabia has the largest reserves of oil in the world and traditionally has been one of the world's largest oil producers. When crude oil is produced, large quantities of natural gas are automatically produced with it. This so-called associated gas provides the major raw materials—methane and ethane—upon which the Saudi petrochemical industry has been built. Additional hydrocarbon feedstock is provided by benzene, made locally by refining Saudi crude oil. The remaining important raw material is salt, which is used to make chlorine, an important feedstock for vinyl chloride monomer. In addition to raw materials, the Saudis had capital, amassed after the oil price increase of 1973.

The government gave responsibility for petrochemical development to the Saudi Basic Industries Corporation (SABIC), formed in 1976, which, in turn, selected foreign partners, principally major petrochemical producers headquartered in the United States, but also some from Japan and South Korea. Planning was started on the Saudi petrochemical complexes in the late 1970s, and construction began in the early 1980s. By the end of 1985, virtually all of the facilities were in operation, with many completed ahead of schedule and under budget. When operating at full capacity, the Saudi petrochemical industry would turn out about $ 2.0 billion yearly of petrochemicals, or less than about 1 percent of the world petrochemical output (see Table 9-1). This market share is substantially below the 5 percent figure that has appeared in the U.S. and European press, presumably because the share of Saudi products was reported as a percentage of only those products made in Saudi Arabia rather than as a percentage of all petrochemicals.

Some of the products being produced in Saudi Arabia are monomers; hence, the product specifications are standardized among all manufacturers. The polymers manufactured there tend to be commodities, with standardized specifications, rather than specialties. Thus, Saudi Arabia has a narrow product line for linear low-density polyethylene (LLDPE), with five commodity-type resins accounting for 80 to 90 percent of output. Gas-rich licensees in Alberta and Argentina have a similar situation. In contrast, the five largest-volume LLDPE resins account for only 40 percent of the very wide product lines of the firms that innovated the technology (Dow and Union Carbide). In sharp contrast to the technology innovators, the gas-rich licensees are not developing new catalysts and new products.[31] The licensees are playing the traditional role of the "manufacturing specialist" mentioned in chapter 4. Their

Table 9-1
Petrochemical Plants in Saudi Arabia, 1985

Petrochemical	Partner	Capacity (1,000 tons a year)	Market Value at Full Capacity ($ millions a year)
Methanol	Japanese consortium	600	
	Celanese/Texas Eastern	650	
	Subtotal	1,250	$180
Urea (from ammonia)	Taiwan Fertilizer	500	
	Saudi investors	330	
	Subtotal	830	120

Table 9-1 Continued

Petrochemical	Partner	Capacity (1,000 tons a year)	Market Value at Full Capacity ($ millions a year)
Ethylene	Shell Oil	656	
	Mobil	455	
	SABIC	500	
	Subtotal	1,611	500
Polyethylene (low-density)[a]	Mobil	205	
	Exxon	270	
	Japanese consortium	130	
	Subtotal	605	410
Polyethylene (high-density)	Mobil	91	50
Ethylene glycol (from ethylene oxide)	Mobil	220	
	Japanese consortium	300	
	Subtotal	520	180
Ethanol	Shell	281	70
Styrene monomer	Shell	295	140
Ethylene dichloride	Shell	454	90
Vinyl chloride monomer (from ethylene dichloride)	Lucky Group (South Korea)	300	100
Polyvinyl chloride	Lucky Group (South Korea)	200	120
			Total $1,960

Note: All plants were onstream in 1985, except the vinyl chloride monomer and polyvinyl chloride plants, which came onstream in 1986.
[a] Can also make high-density polyethylene.
Source: Douglas Smock, "The Saudis Are Coming," CPI Purchasing, March 1985, pp. 46–51, except market values calculated by author from unit values obtained from U.S. International Trade Commission, Synthetic Organic Chemicals—U.S. Production and Sales, 1985 (Washington, DC: GPO, 1986). Ethanol figure is from 1984 report since it was not reported in the 1985 report.

major competitive weapon is a low manufacturing cost due to low raw material and energy costs and large-scale modern plants. These low costs can be translated into low prices if necessary to obtain sales.

In spite of the Saudis' low-cost strategy, their planners took great pains to have the products sold with a minimum of disruption in existing markets. SABIC selected its foreign partners partially on the basis of their markets and marketing skills. The foreign partners agreed to market 50 to 100 percent of the production until SABIC developed its own marketing capabilities. As one item in an emphasis on not disturbing markets, the foreign partners agreed to close some of their own capacity in order to make room for the products from Saudi Arabia. Furthermore, plans were made to spread the products among a number of different world markets, and SABIC promised not to gain market share by cutting prices.

In spite of these precautions, Saudi products received a warm reception in the industrialized countries only in Japan, where some plants had been closed to make way for Saudi material. Saudi petrochemicals received a cooler reception in the United States, where normal tariffs were imposed and where some politicians talked of additional trade barriers against "subsidized" imports. In Europe, the situation was even more complicated. The European Economic Community's imports from Saudi Arabia are governed by the generalized system of preferences (GSP) for developing countries. Under this system, Saudi Arabia is allowed a fixed quantity of duty-free exports to the EEC, with normal EEC tariffs imposed on the rest. In practice, the Europeans routinely waive tariffs on the things they want to buy, like refined oil products. The Saudis apparently expected that their exports of petrochemicals to the EEC would be duty-free. Instead, after a period of some confusion, the EEC began to apply their normal duties automatically as soon as the imports from Saudi Arabia exceeded the Saudi quotas, which were so low as to be called "derisory"—about one day's output of Saudi methanol, for example.[32]

Still, a considerable portion of the Saudi output has entered the European market. In 1987, the Association of Petrochemical Producers in Europe estimated that Middle East imports, mainly from Saudi Arabia, had a 20 to 25 percent share of the methanol, ethylene glycol, and styrene markets and 10 to 15 percent of the linear low-density polyethylene and high-density polyethylene sectors in Europe.[33]

Given the wide interest in the buildup of petrochemical facilities in hydrocarbon-rich countries and the great concern over the U.S. trade deficit, a closer look at U.S. trade in petrochemicals is justified.

U.S. Trade. Other than in methanol and ammonia, the buildup in petrochemical facilities in hydrocarbon-rich countries seems to have had little effect on U.S. trade patterns. U.S. exports of petrochemicals in 1973 were a little more than 10 percent of U.S. output. After the 1973 jump in world oil prices, U.S. price controls on crude oil and natural gas had the effect of subsidizing U.S. exports, which grew to more than 16 percent of U.S. output in 1980. A side effect was that foreign companies bought subsidized U.S. petrochemicals (paraxylene, for example) and used them to make products with which they penetrated the U.S. market (fibers, for example). With the end of oil price controls in 1981 and phase-out of some natural-gas price controls through 1985, U.S. petrochemical manufacturers lost a cost advantage over their foreign competitors. This, combined with a rise in the exchange rate value of the dollar, contributed to a decline in exports. U.S. exports of petrochemical products declined to a little more than 12 percent of U.S. petrochemical output in 1985, still quite a respectable showing given all the negative factors (see Figure 9-3).

The export performance recorded for the nine products during the post-1973 period was also respectable. A new export peak, measured in absolute volume, was reached for seven of the products and a new export peak, measured as a percentage of U.S. production, was attained for three. In fact, exports of the nine products as a percentage of U.S. production, which had declined from an average of 17 percent in 1961 to 12 percent in 1973, had increased to 14 percent by 1985.

As was the case before 1973, there was no evidence that U.S. exports would gradually fade to zero as production commenced in more countries. The need for exports to balance supply and demand in a number of countries at any given time still existed and in some cases was growing, despite widespread belief to the contrary. For example, the trade press in early 1985 reported that U.S.

Figure 9-3

U.S. Exports and Imports of All Petrochemical Products, 1973–1985

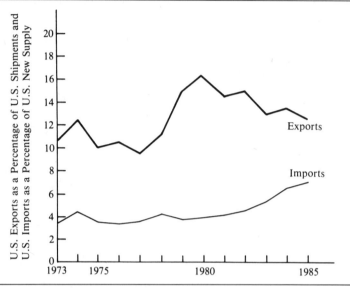

Sources: U.S. Department of Commerce, *U.S. Industrial Outlook* (Washington, DC: GPO), 1986, p. 11-2 and 1987, p. 11-4.

exports of styrene monomer would decline from 1,170 million pounds in 1984 to 650–700 million pounds in 1985 due to increases in world capacity.[34] In fact, U.S. exports in 1985 increased to 1,330 million pounds.

The negative factors mentioned above did manage to make a showing, however small, in the U.S. import picture. Between 1973 and 1981, U.S. imports of petrochemicals had been about 4 percent of U.S. new supply. This number began to rise in 1982 and reached almost 7 percent in 1985 (see Figure 9-3), with the strong dollar being a major reason for the increase. This was an important trend, but the increase was still small (about $3.2 billion) compared to the $100 billion increase in U.S. imports of manufactured goods between 1982 and 1985. Overall, the U.S. net trade surplus in petrochemicals dropped from $9 billion in 1980 to a little less than $5 billion in 1985.[35]

This reduction in the positive balance of trade, combined with the experience of the years 1973–1985, has raised the question

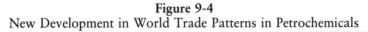

Figure 9-4
New Development in World Trade Patterns in Petrochemicals

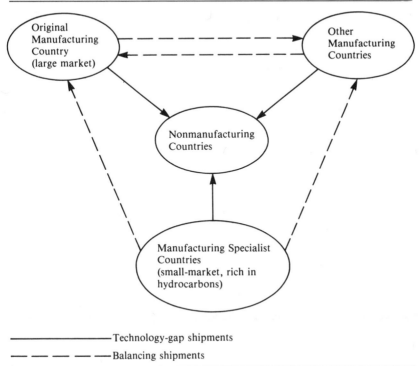

——————————————Technology-gap shipments

— — — — — ——Balancing shipments

Note: For earlier patterns, see Figure 7-2.

whether a new world trade pattern will supplant previous patterns
(illustrated in Figure 7-2). This new pattern continues to have
balancing shipments among countries manufacturing the product
and technology-gap shipments to nonproducing countries (see Figure 9-4). What is new is the resource-dependent trade; that is,
balancing shipments and technology-gap shipments from export-
dependent plants in small-market countries rich in hydrocarbons.

Because of this new pattern, there is apprehension throughout
the industrialized countries that their previously favorable trade
balance in petrochemicals will turn negative and their petrochemical industry will be badly damaged. In the United States, for example, the U.S. International Trade Commission predicted that the
U.S. net trade balance in petrochemicals would disappear by 1990

and that the United States would become a net importer. And the head of the Office of Productivity, Technology & Innovation of the U.S. Department of Commerce predicted that "We have about $80 billion of commodity petrochemicals in the U.S., and we are going to lose these in the next period of years, and the only uncertainty is how fast."[36] The implications of this new trend in production and trade are vital so I address the issue in the following chapter.

CHAPTER 10

A LOOK AHEAD

Peering into the future is always a perilous undertaking, but it is important in order to frame future policies.

The industry will not return to the freewheeling days of the golden era, when innovation reduced costs and spurred market growth sufficiently to mitigate the mistake of adding too much capacity too quickly. Nevertheless, the dramatic drop in world oil prices in 1986 sprinkled benefits on the petrochemical industry, particularly in the energy-importing industrialized countries, where most petrochemicals are made and consumed. Lower oil prices contributed to an increase in general economic activity, resulting in higher consumption of petrochemicals. Furthermore, lower oil prices pulled natural gas prices below levels that would otherwise have existed. The combination of lower oil and gas prices reduced petrochemical costs, part of which have been passed on to consumers through lower prices and part of which have been retained by producers as higher profits. Although oil prices are bound to be unstable, any increases are likely to be restrained for quite some time.

The results of the lower oil and petrochemical prices will be reflected in three major areas: the petrochemical industry, company strategies, and government policies.

INDUSTRY CHANGES

Continuing uncertainties confront the industry with respect to trade patterns, market growth, and innovation.

Trade Patterns

The decline in petrochemical prices has cut the profits of the export-dependent petrochemical plants in the hydrocarbon-rich countries. Still, the marginal costs of the plants will remain less than those of plants in the industrialized countries because most of the marginal costs of plants in the hydrocarbon-rich countries consist of prices for methane and ethane. Methane is used for energy, and both methane and ethane are the principal raw materials in the production of petrochemicals in these countries. If necessary, the governments of these nations will lower the prices of methane and ethane rather than let plants sit idle while the gases are flared. It is unlikely, therefore, that lower oil prices will prevent export-dependent plants in hydrocarbon-rich countries from shipping to the industrialized nations.

These shipments, while small relative to the markets of the industrialized countries, can have a significant effect on prices: A domestic purchaser with the opportunity to buy imported products can use the lower prices of the imports to squeeze down the prices of domestic suppliers. Commenting on paraxylene imports into the United States, one trade journal said, "Like the small stones that trigger a landslide, the trickle of paraxylene imports that is due to enter the country at prices below the current domestic average during the next forty-five days has begun to make its presence felt with a force out of proportion to its size."[1] In this case, the imports in question amounted to less than 1 percent of U.S. paraxylene consumption that year, yet domestic producers responded by cutting prices. And in Europe, the price of low-density polyethylene dropped 16 percent in the fall of 1984 in anticipation of imports from Saudi Arabia as companies fought for market position.[2]

Although the marginal costs of making petrochemicals in an existing facility in a hydrocarbon-rich country are low, the cost of building a new facility in these countries is generally quite high. As a result, the reduced profit potential of petrochemicals combined with the dramatically lower income due to the lower oil prices has had a chilling effect on those countries' plans to expand petrochemical production facilities. The construction slowdown in hydrocarbon-rich countries will have a favorable effect on producers in the industrialized countries. Accordingly, in general, apprehension that the favorable petrochemical trade balance of the industrialized countries will disappear is unfounded. It is difficult to make predictions for specific countries because of the sensitivity of petrochemical trade to currency changes. But if the U.S. dollar does not rise above its mid-1987 level relative to other currencies, the bleak forecast by the United States International Trade Commission that the positive U.S. trade balance in petrochemicals would disappear by 1990 will not be realized. Indeed, a modest improvement in the U.S. petrochemical trade balance in 1986 supports a more optimistic view.[3] It is unlikely that the U.S. positive trade balance in petrochemicals will drop below the $4 to $6 billion range unless there are major economic changes not now foreseeable.

Market Growth

Lower petrochemical prices will cause petrochemical consumption to grow slightly faster than GNP in the industrialized countries, at least until markets for the products mature further.[4] This growth rate will be considerably higher than that which prevailed during the transition years 1973–1985. On the other hand, it will be considerably lower than that which existed during the golden era prior to 1973, when market growth in the United States was three times that of GNP and even more abroad. Most analysts agree that in the developing countries consumption growth will easily exceed GNP growth, but will have only a modest influence on the overall picture, since most consumption is concentrated in the industrialized countries.

The overall growth may attract new entrants into the industry, but even if this occurs, the number will be small and nothing like the mass entry that took place before 1973.[5] Therefore, competition is unlikely to become so severe as to cause a repetition of the losses experienced in the early 1980s.[6]

Innovation

Whatever happens to oil prices, the large domestic markets of the industrialized nations will continue to provide them with a major advantage in innovating new chemical products.[7] Four critical changes, however, have occurred that will probably alter the future pattern of innovation of all new products, including chemicals, in the industrialized nations.[8]

First, over the past few decades, the markets of the industrialized countries have become much more similar. In the major European countries, per capita incomes have risen to approximate that of the United States—the original producer of most new petrochemicals commercialized since World War II. Japan's per capita income also has reached the U.S. level. Moreover, the formation and subsequent enlargement of the European Economic Community has created a market with a population and GNP even larger than those of the United States.

Second, differences in production costs have become less pronounced. With higher wages, firms in Europe and Japan now have a strong incentive to develop labor-saving innovations. In the United States, higher energy costs and a growing share of imported raw materials have led to a greater incentive to develop energy- and material-saving innovations.

Third, multinational enterprises have gained experience in foreign environments, spreading their networks into many more countries, thereby reducing uncertainty about opportunities for innovating new products abroad.[9]

Fourth, although most products are still developed initially for a home market, vastly improved communication technology has made it easier to innovate a product in one country and commercialize it in another. Both multinational and national firms are affected by this development.

As a result of these four changes, innovation patterns should differ less among industrialized nations in the future than in the past. Still, the United States should have some advantage over

Japan because the U.S. market is clearly the larger of the two. The United States should also have some advantage over Europe because the U.S. market is much more homogeneous than the European.

In spite of the growing pool of nations and firms in the industrialized world capable of introducing new products, the long-term decline in innovation that has been occurring in petrochemicals suggests that, in fact, relatively few new petrochemical products will be commercialized. Furthermore, even with the growth expected in the industry, the slowdown in the rate of process innovation in existing products is apt to continue, and the relatively few process innovations that do occur are likely to be minor rather than major.[10]

COMPANY STRATEGIES

Company managers will have to frame new strategies in order to cope with the forgoing developments in the petrochemical industry. Moreover, in view of the sluggish growth expected in the markets for conventional petrochemicals, managers are likely to seek new opportunities in specialty chemicals.

Conventional Petrochemicals

Depending on the product line, successful companies will adopt one of two basic strategies to achieve a competitive advantage: product differentiation or low cost.[11]

In some lines, companies will continue to differentiate products by developing new grades of existing plastics, fibers, and elastomers, and will continue to provide technical support and application development. Sustaining a competitive advantage, of course, requires continual change to ensure providing what buyers value. In some product lines, for instance, opportunities for product differentiation and special service will diminish to such an extent that a firm will have to use a low-cost strategy. Indeed, this has already occurred in a number of product lines.

The second strategy, achieving a low-cost position, requires improving the productivity of personnel, obtaining low-cost raw materials, and processing them efficiently, if necessary with purchased technology. Low costs are important for long-run survival, for high-cost producers will be very vulnerable during cyclical downturns. In some cases, a corporation, especially when it cannot add value above and beyond what could be achieved if its business units were independent, will sell some of the businesses. Often, a commodity business will be sold to a "manufacturing specialist," who then will concentrate on reducing costs. For example, Vista Chemical, a company formed to buy out some of Du Pont's commodity chemical businesses, reduced nonplant costs by some 20 percent below the target previously set by Du Pont.[12]

Regardless of which strategy they use, firms will be reluctant to build new plants, especially for commodity operations not in hydrocarbon-rich countries. For most products, even the improved profit margins that existed in 1987 were a long way below the margins needed to justify the construction of new facilities. True, profit margins might improve substantially given the relatively high plant utilization rates existing in 1987. But these utilization rates will not necessarily continue because demand will be cyclical, depending on the health of the general economy. Moreover, it is possible that some of the capacity closed earlier in the decade will be re-started.[13] And there is the specter of competition from the hydrocarbon-rich countries, since a substantial increase in oil and gas prices will encourage building new facilities in these countries. Therefore, it appears that for quite some time most new capacity will come from debottlenecking rather than from new plants.

Firms, of course, will select a mix of strategies for their various product lines on the basis of their competitive advantages and disadvantages in each of the lines. The successful implementation of one or more of these strategies should help petrochemical firms to increase earnings, but there seems to be no course that ensures a bright long-term future in conventional petrochemicals. Growth and earnings in the petrochemical industry have been invigorated by innovation, and that source, if not running dry, is providing much less than in the past. Managers in the petrochemical industry must look elsewhere for innovation opportunities. "Elsewhere" is, of course, in specialty chemicals. While it is true that many, perhaps most, specialty chemicals are made from oil or gas raw materials, and so can technically be considered "petrochemicals," the dominating feature of specialty chemicals is the effort necessary to achieve the high value added rather than the raw materials from which they are made.

The Allure of Specialty Chemicals

Specialty chemicals are not new. Many of today's commodity chemicals, including conventional petrochemicals, started out as specialty products decades ago. Yet there is still no precise, widely accepted definition of specialty chemicals. Observers agree only that whereas commodity chemicals are purchased in large volumes on the basis of specifications, and with price as the overwhelming consideration, specialty chemicals are purchased in small quantities on the basis of performance, and with service as an important factor. There is no commonly accepted categorization of specialty chemicals, as some groupings are based on the type of product and others on the industry in which the products are used. Given the problems of definition, it is not surprising that the precise size of the market for specialty chemicals is unknown. Still, it is safe to say that the world market probably exceeds $100 billion—or perhaps a third or so the size of the petrochemical industry.[14]

The market for specialty chemicals is overwhelmingly concentrated in the industrialized countries, split among the three major areas approximately as follows: United States, 45 percent; Western Europe, 35 percent; and Japan, 15 percent.[15] The specialty chemicals industry in the industrialized countries is expected to grow for many years at a rate of perhaps twice that of GNP, or considerably more than that of the conventional petrochemical industry. It is foreseen that a number of categories of specialty chemicals will expand at three times or more the rate of GNP. The categories include electronic chemicals used to make microchips, diagnostic reagents, synthetic lubricants, and advanced new materials, including high-performance polymers, composites, and ceramics.[16]

Profits of U.S. specialty chemical companies have been very attractive, averaging 15 percent return on invested capital between

1973 and 1985, compared with 8 percent for U.S. basic chemical companies, including petrochemical producers. Any attempt, however, to shift from the disciplines imposed by the petrochemical markets to those of the specialty chemical markets faces certain difficulties.[17]

First, achieving success in specialties requires a different set of skills from those required in conventional petrochemicals, especially the basics and intermediates. Whereas the conventional petrochemical business is geared toward engineering and operations, the specialty chemicals business relies heavily on marketing and product development. This obstacle is not insurmountable, since a number of petrochemical firms have shown that they either already have the required skills or can develop them. Many petrochemical companies already employ scientists, engineers, and marketing people with experience relevant to the development of specialty chemicals.

The second barrier to petrochemical firms entering the specialties business is that petrochemical firms tend to be large, hierarchical organizations that emphasize engineering and production. In contrast, specialty chemical companies tend to be small, flexible organizations that emphasize R&D and marketing. Here, entrepreneurial spirit is a necessity, for decisions must be made quickly on incomplete information. Therefore, the specialty chemicals and conventional petrochemical businesses are not natural bedfellows. On the other hand, as discussed in chapter 4, large firms do have an overall advantage in the innovation of new petrochemical products. The challenge for the large companies is to learn to develop an organization that simulates the entrepreneurial environment that is found in many small organizations.[18]

The third drawback is the fact that total sales of specialty chemicals are considerably smaller than sales of conventional petrochemicals; indeed, one view suggests that petrochemical companies will be unable to achieve a large enough position in specialties to make a difference in their overall corporate position.[19] This view, however, overemphasizes the existing market without considering the potential rapid growth in specialties if substantial research, development, and marketing efforts are made.

Indeed, some firms have made great progress in moving into the specialty chemical business. By 1986, for example, the specialty chemical businesses of Monsanto, Dow Chemical, and Imperial

Chemical Industries were equal to, or larger than, their conventional petrochemical businesses.[20]

A DIRECTION FOR GOVERNMENT POLICIES

Government policies are so heavily influenced by political events that making accurate forecasts in this area is particularly difficult. Therefore, in lieu of making predictions about government policies, I provide some directions in which governments in the industrialized countries might go to enable their petrochemical industries to develop in a manner consistent with the national welfare. The policies discussed below embrace protectionism, environmental and worker health regulations, and the ever vital area of innovation.

Protectionism

It seems likely that in the industrial nations government policies concerning petrochemicals will continue to focus on imports, particularly those from the hydrocarbon-rich countries. Indeed, any cyclical fluctuations in demand that lead to reduced profit margins and possible losses for the high-cost producers in these countries will elicit further charges of unfair trade practices leveled against foreign producers rich in oil and gas. The fact is that neither the United States, Western Europe, nor Japan is in any danger of losing its commodity petrochemical industry. Most of the closures that have occurred thus far were due to overbuilding by domestic firms rather than to imports.[21]

Import protection for petrochemicals is not a rational policy for industrialized countries because it encourages domestic producers to compete against producers in countries with a significant comparative advantage in raw-material costs. Moreover, these competitors can readily purchase state-of-the-art technology.[22] And, import protection is bound to encourage firms to focus on the domestic market and thereby fail to provide capacity for "balancing exports" to countries already producing the product.[23]

There are three arguments for import protection that may have general economic merit, but none seem to apply to the petrochemical industry in the industrialized countries.[24]

The first of these arguments is concerned with an infant industry in a developing country, where protection may be desirable until the industry can compete with imports. This situation does not exist in industrialized countries, most of which already have well-established petrochemical industries.

The second argument is that limiting imports prevents plant shutdowns and therefore preserves employment. But limiting imports leads to higher prices for petrochemicals. Higher prices, in turn, damage the petrochemical-consuming industries, where employment is greater than in petrochemicals.[25] In order to encourage employment in the overall economy, it is ordinarily more effective for a government to concentrate on monetary and fiscal policies rather than to single out an individual industry for protection. Indeed, protecting individual industries often results in a very high cost for each job saved. For example, Gary Hufbauer and colleagues at the Institute for International Economics estimated that the special protection granted to U.S. producers of certain chemicals comprising a very small part of the overall industry cost U.S. consumers over $1 million for each job saved.[26]

The third economic rationale for import protection is to improve the terms of trade in favor of the importing country against the exporting country; in other words, to cause the hydrocarbon-rich countries to sell petrochemicals to the industrialized countries at a lower price than they otherwise would. Even though tariffs accomplish this to some extent, any savings on the relatively small quantities of imports from these nations are likely to be offset by higher petrochemical prices that would exist in the industrialized countries that have import protection.

Of course, if the industrialized nations allow access to their markets, then they have the right to expect similar access to the markets of others.

Environmental and Worker Health Regulation

Governments obviously are responsible for protecting the environment and workers from the negative effects of chemicals.[27] But the increased focus of governments on this issue is creating concerns about the possible inhibiting effects on innovation. There is some fear, for example, that proliferation of registration requirements by state and local governments in the United States is unduly inhibiting the commercialization of new chemical products. The problem could be somewhat alleviated if federal mandates, particularly where data collection and labeling are concerned, preempted state and local laws. There is also fear that regulations, such as the Toxic Substance Control Act (TSCA), are unduly inhibiting the commercialization of new chemical products in the United States, because of the elaborate steps required to obtain approval for a new product.[28] On the other hand, there is concern that lax waste-disposal regulations in other countries will encourage the location of such facilities in those countries.

International agreements could help ensure that nations do not compete with each other by fouling the environment, especially when fouling one's own environment often involves polluting a neighbor's as well. Such international agreements might be reached initially through the Organization for Economic Cooperation and Development, and later, a larger body. It may take a long time for such agreements to be reached, but a start is necessary if any progress is to be made. The international agreement covering maritime wastes is a good example of what can be accomplished.[29]

Innovation

Innovation can contribute to the welfare of a country, particularly new-product innovation in the large-market industrialized countries, for this is an area in which they have a natural comparative advantage. For one thing, product innovation requires highly skilled, and highly paid, persons such as scientists, engineers, marketing executives, and general managers. Furthermore, to the extent that product innovation generates monopoly and oligopoly profits for the innovating firm, it also contributes to the national income. And not least, the competitive lead of the nation in which the development occurs is reflected in the large amounts of product exports it achieves—much more than if the product is first commercialized elsewhere.[30]

Although product innovation is likely to result in the highest returns for the industrialized nations, process innovation can also help generate a high national income. The nation in which the innovation occurs gains from the export of process technology. Even if the technology is not exported, the nation can profit from the export of lower-cost products made with the new technology.

Industrialized countries can encourage innovation by helping create larger markets. One way is to support the creation of one homogeneous market rather than a number of heterogeneous ones. Countries in the European Economic Community, for instance, need to continue to work on common standards and to eliminate nontariff barriers.[31] The United States needs nationwide building codes and safety regulations.

Another way of encouraging innovation is to modify the General Agreement on Tariffs and Trade (GATT). This agreement, focused on guaranteeing fair international trade in goods, should be changed to break down barriers to foreign investment, to include trade in technology, and to improve the protection and enforcement of intellectual property rights. A revised GATT would help ensure that innovating firms have the option of either using their technology or of selling it anywhere in the world.[32]

A third way to encourage innovation is to extend the effective patent life for new products by having that life start with any government approval required for commercial manufacture, rather than when the patent is granted. In the United States, for example, the patent life would not begin until the government had granted any approval required under TSCA.

Even more direct government intervention is possible. Fiscal policies to subsidize capital expenditures by private industry are often mentioned. But such subsidization should not come at the expense of investments in innovation. Indeed, economic theory indicates that governments should subsidize innovation by individual firms, because if a firm fails to benefit from knowledge it creates, such knowledge can still be of use to society. In practice, however, the difficulties in implementing a government subsidy program often result in very high costs; a recent study of several countries, including the United States, suggests that governments have granted a tax benefit of $3 for every extra $1 of R&D stimulated. There does seem, however, to be a widespread belief that generic research support is likely to be a successful type of government R&D program.[33]

Other possibilities of direct intervention that have been mentioned include the formation of R&D consortia and monitoring foreign commercial developments.[34] But given the speed with which changes occur, it is not clear that governments would have an advantage over individual firms or groups of firms in performing such activities.

Other than support of generic-type research, the recent experience of the petrochemical industry suggests that it is undesirable for governments of industrialized countries to alter artificially the economic patterns in the industry. Market forces work well. Indeed, neither tariff protection nor national industrial planning is needed for this industry. A more rational approach would be to remove artificial barriers that might prevent companies from moving resources into the higher value-added activities in which the industrialized countries have a major advantage—innovation of new chemical products.

Important Characteristics of the Petrochemical Industry

	Market Characteristics
Product differentiation	Specialties, which are products sold on the basis of performance, differentiated; commodities, which are products sold on the basis of well-defined characteristics, not differentiated[1]
Size of total market	Worldwide output approximating $300 to $350 billion; the United States and Western Europe each producing about one-third of the total, with the remainder split in more or less equal shares between Japan, the Centrally Planned Economies, and the rest of the world (principally the developing countries); any single petrochemical accounting for a small share of total[2]
Number of sellers and buyers	Sellers of a particular product typically few enough in number to constitute an oligopoly, but with more sellers of commodities than of specialties; typically more buyers than sellers[3]
Barriers to entry	Technology in early years of product's life, scale economies in later years[4]
Vertical integration	Some vertical integration between raw materials and petrochemicals and between some petrochemicals; less vertical integration between petrochemicals and products made from petrochemicals[5]
Conglomerateness	Each petrochemical made by a slightly different set of manufacturers from every other petrochemical, with some overlap in members of different sets; parent companies from many different industries—mostly oil and chemicals, but also steel, rubber, and others; most manufacturers make a number of different petrochemicals[6]

(continued)

Appendix A (continued)

	Supply
Raw materials	Petroleum products from crude oil and natural gas[7]
Technology	Some batch, but mostly continuous process facilities that are highly automated and capital-intensive, with large economies of scale[8]
Work force	Proportion of engineers and scientists to workers greater than the average in manufacturing[9]
Value/weight	Cost of transporting a petrochemical typically small compared with its price[10]
Research and innovation	One of leading spenders on research and development and on output of innovations compared with other industries[11]
Efficiency and progress	High rate of productivity growth compared with other industries[12]
	Demand
Nature of end product	A liquid or a solid that can be further processed in one or more steps into final products most often made from plastics, synthetic fibers, or synthetic rubbers[13]
Price elasticity	Low for specialties, and high for commodities—with specialty status most often occurring in early years of product's life and commodity status most often occurring in later years [14]
Substitutes	Final products made from petrochemicals competing in many separate markets, sometimes with one another and sometimes with products made from such natural materials as wood, leather, silk, cotton, wool, rubber, steel, aluminum, glass, and paper[15]
Rate of growth	High during early years of a product's life and low during later years[16]
Length of product's life	Can be 60 years or more[17]
Cyclical aspects	Correlated with business cycle—especially the commodities[18]

NOTES

1. See Robert B. Stobaugh, *Petrochemical Manufacturing and Marketing Guide*, vols. 1 and 2 (Houston: Gulf Publishing, 1966 and 1968); Frederick A. Lowenheim and Marguerite K. Moran, *Faith, Keyes, and Clark's Industrial Chemicals*, 4th ed. (New York: Wiley, 1975); Robert B. Stobaugh and Phillip L. Townsend, "Price Forecasting and Strategic Planning: The Case of Petrochemicals," *Journal of Marketing Research* February 1975, pp. 19–29. United States International Trade Commission, *The Shift from U.S. Production of Commodity Petrochemicals to Value-Added Specialty Chemical Products and the Possible Impact on U.S. Trade*, USITC Publication 1677 (Washington, DC: GPO, April 1985); and interviews with marketing executives.

2. See note 7, chapter 1.

3. See note 1.

4. Robert B. Stobaugh, *Petrochemical Manufacturing and Marketing Guide*, vols. 1 and 2; Lowenheim and Moran, *Faith, Keyes, and Clark's Industrial Chemicals;* Robert Stobaugh, "Channels for Technology Transfer: The Petrochemical Industry." In *Technology Crossing Borders*, ed. Robert Stobaugh and Louis T. Wells, Jr., (Boston: Harvard Business School Press, 1984), pp. 157–176.

5. Robert B. Stobaugh, *Petrochemical Manufacturing and Marketing Guide*, vols. 1 and 2; Lowenheim and Moran, *Faith, Keyes, and Clark's Industrial Chemicals*.

6. Ibid.

7. Ibid.

8. Ibid.

9. U.S. Bureau of Labor Statistics, *Employment of Scientific and Technical Personnel in Industry, 1962*, Bull. No. 1418 (Washington, DC: GPO, 1964) and *Employment and Earnings Statistics for the United States, 1909–46* (Washington, DC: GPO, 1965).

10. Correspondence with companies.

11. For R&D expenditures, see Richard R. Nelson and Sidney G. Winter, "In Search of a Useful Theory of Innovation," *Research Policy* (January 1977), p. 39. For innovation, see A. Wade Blockman, Edward J. Seligman, and Gene G. Sogliero, "An Innovation Index Based on Factor Analysis," *Technological Forecasting and Social Change*, 1973, pp. 201–316.

12. Productivity growth in the U.S. manufacturing sector (of 23 industries) was highest for chemicals in terms of percentage yearly increases in total factory productivity and output per worker. See J. Kendrick, quoted in Nelson and Winter, "In Search of a Useful Theory of Innovation," p. 39, Tables 5.1 and 5.5.

13. See note 5.

14. See note 1.

15. See note 5.

16. See note 5, plus U.S. International Trade Commission, *Synthetic Organic Chemicals—U.S. Production and Sales,* various years.

17. Ibid.

18. U.S. Department of Commerce, *U.S. Industrial Outlook* (Washington, DC: GPO), various years.

APPENDIX B

Petrochemical Industry Relationships

PETROCHEMICAL FEEDSTOCKS OR RAW MATERIALS	PETROCHEMICAL INDUSTRY MATERIALS			PETROCHEMICAL-DEPENDENT PRODUCTS
	Primaries	Intermediates	Products	
Petroleum Liquids	*Aromatics*	*Aromatic/cyclic*	Plastic Materials	Fabricated Plastic Products
Naphtha	Benzene	Ethylbenzene	e.g., polystyrene	e.g., molded products
Reformate	Toluene	Styrene*	Synthetic Rubbers	Fabricated Rubber Products
Raffinate	Xylenes (mixed)	Phenol*	e.g., polybutadiene	e.g., tires, tubes
Gas oil	o-Xylene*	Phthalic Anhydride	Synthetic Fibers	Textile Mill Products
Carbon black oil	m-Xylene	Terephthalic Acid	e.g., nylon	e.g., woven fabrics
Crude oil	p-Xylene*	Aniline	Surfactants	Cleaning Preparations
Still gas	Naphthalene	Cyclohexane*	e.g., arylsulfonates	e.g., soap & detergents
LRG/Gas				Mixed Fertilizers
				e.g., mixtures of N.P.K.
Natural Gas Liquids	*Olefins-Unsaturates*	*Aliphatic/acyclic*	Nitrogenous Fertilizers	Drugs
Ethane	Ethylene	Acetic Acid	e.g., ammonium nitrate	e.g., pharmaceuticals
Propane	Propylene	Ethylene Oxide	Phosphatic Fertilizers	Coatings
Butanes	Butylene	Ethylene Glycol	e.g., ammonium phosphate	e.g., paints, lacquers
LPG	Butadiene	Ethylene Dichloride	Pesticides	Explosives
Natural gasoline	Acetylene	Vinyl Chloride*	e.g., malathion	e.g., blasting compounds
	Isoprene*	Formaldehyde		
		Butanol		
	Methanol*	Acrylonitrile*		
Gases				
Methane	Ammonia			
Synthesis gas				
Still gas	Carbon Black			
Standard Industrial Codes (SICs): 2911	2865, 2869, 2895		2821, 2822, 2824, 2843, 2873	2823, 2831, 2833, 2834, 2841, 2842, 2844, 2851, 2874, 2875, 2879, 2891, 2892, 2893

* One of the nine products studied in detail, see chapter 1.

Source: *A Competitive Assessment of the U.S. Petrochemical Industry* (Washington, DC: U.S. Department of Commerce, Office of Competitive Assessment, August 31, 1982. Report Number DOC/OCA-83/001), p. 2, with cyclohexane, isoprene, and acrylonitrile added by author.

A Brief History of the Petrochemical Industry

The groundwork for the petrochemical industry was laid during the nineteenth century, when Germany, Great Britain, and France gave birth to the modern organic chemical industry (most petrochemicals are organic chemicals; that is, they contain one or more carbon atoms). For raw materials, the firms used coal-tar by-products from nearby iron and steel plants. During this time, an especially important organic chemical was artificial synthetic dyestuff, which German firms took the lead in developing on a large-scale, commercial basis. This advantage gave Germany a head start in the organic chemical industry that was not overcome until well into the next century.[1]

Wars were to play important roles in the development of the organic chemical industry. World War I had two lasting impacts on it. First, with the cutoff in the supply of German organic chemicals, the American industry grew dramatically. In addition, World War I played a key role in the actual birth of the petrochemical industry. The war created a demand for large amounts of the organic chemical acetone to produce explosives. In 1916, in response to this demand, Carlton Ellis, a chemist and inventor, discovered a method for using petroleum raw materials to make isopropyl alcohol, a raw material used in the manufacture of acetone. The war ended before isopropyl alcohol could play a role, but Standard Oil of New Jersey (now Exxon) decided to add it to gasoline as an extender, in face of the potential shortage of crude oil that many foresaw. In 1919, the company acquired the Ellis patents and constructed the world's first large petrochemical plant at Bayway, NJ.[2]

In the period between World War I and World War II, when additional groundwork was laid for periods of enormous expansion, certain trends that characterized the petrochemical industry began to emerge.[3]

First, oil and natural gas gradually began to supplement—and later supplant—coal tar as a raw material for chemicals, particularly organic chemicals.

Second, many new petrochemical products were commercialized, including such solids as polystyrene, polyvinyl chloride, polyethylene, and nylon, which began to substitute for natural materials, such as wood, leather, silk, cotton, wool, rubber, steel, aluminum, glass, and paper.

Third, competition increased. True, there was a consolidation (through mergers) to form I.G. Farben in Germany and Imperial Chemical Industries in Great Britain. Further, Imperial Chemical Industries had some technology-sharing agreements with Du Pont. Any reduction in competition, however, was short-lived as other chemical companies, as well as major firms in other industries, especially petroleum and rubber. began manufacturing petrochemicals.

With the advent of World War II, the need for synthetics to substitute for natural materials, especially rubber, which was imported from the Far East, caused governments to take an active hand in financing the buildup of the industry. In the United States, such facilities were eventually sold to private companies. In addition, other key factors converged to make U.S. petrochemical companies world leaders. These factors included the destruction of many of the German facilities during the war; the breakup of Germany's giant I.G. Farben into separate companies (including Badische Anilin- & Soda -Fabrik [BASF], Bayer, and Hoechst); the availability of German technology to non-German firms; a large R&D base in the United States; the rapid development of the U.S. oil and gas industry; and the large and affluent American market.

The 1950s and 1960s were a golden era for petrochemicals, marked by expanding markets worldwide, cheap raw materials, and dramatically improved productivity resulting from new processes and large-scale plants. Although other nations began to close the production gap, the U.S. industry continued to occupy a favored position because the large and affluent U.S. market made new product innovation very attractive. In raw materials, the competitive position of the United States, although ambiguous, was better than that of the other industrialized countries, on the average. The U.S. petrochemical manufacturers were unique in having available large supplies of by-product ethane and propane that resulted from the necessary removal of propane and butane from the natural gas transported in the long-distance pipelines. Ethane and propane provided cheaper fuel and raw material for some petrochemicals than were available in Europe or Japan. But because U.S. oil import quotas kept U.S. oil prices higher than those in the world market, U.S. producers had a disadvantage in refinery products (principally naphtha), used by necessity as a raw material to manufacture benzene—another key building block—and by option as a feedstock to manufacture ethylene and propylene. The U.S. petrochemical producers gained some relief from this competitive disadvantage in the late 1960s, when they obtained special quotas for imported oil to use as petrochemical feedstock.[4]

The golden era, characterized by rapid growth in markets, cheap raw material, and a high level of technological innovation, was brought to a sudden end by the 1973 oil shock. Events since that time are covered in chapter 9.

NOTES

1. Ernst Baumler, *Ein Jahrhundert Chemie* (Düsseldorf: Econ-Verlag, 1963), and Wilhelm Vershofen, *Die Anfänge der chemisch-pharmazeutischen Industrie*, vols. 1 and 3 (Berlin: Deutscher Betriebswirte-Verlag, 1949); Archibald Clow and N. L. Clow, *The Chemical Revolution* (London: Batchworth, 1952); L. F. Haber, *The Chemical Industry during the Nineteenth Century* (Oxford: Clarendon Press, 1958); P. M. Hohenberg, *Chemicals in Western Europe: 1850–1914* (Chicago: Rand-McNally, 1967).

2. *Hydrocarbon Processing*, January 1959, p. 179.

3. Note 2 plus Ernst Bäumler, *A Century of Chemistry* (Düsseldorf: Econ-Verlag, 1968); Alexander Findlay, *A Hundred Years of Chemistry* (London: Duckworth, 1937); I. F. Haber, *The Chemical Industry 1900–1930* (Oxford: Clarendon Press, 1971); and Trevor I. Williams, ed., *A History of Technology*, vol. V, *The Twentieth Century c. 1900–c. 1950* (Oxford: Clarendon Press, 1978).

4. Robert B. Stobaugh, "The U.S. Oil Import Program and the Petrochemical Industry," A Report to President Nixon's Cabinet Task Force on Oil Import Control, December 1969 (Washington, DC: National Archives, Submission #SM15) (mimeographed).

The Nine Products

Product	Principal Raw Materials	Principal Uses
Acrylonitrile	Propylene (from ethane, propane, naphtha, or refinery offgas) and ammonia (from natural gas or naphtha)	Fibers and plastics
Cyclohexane	Benzene (from naphtha) and hydrogen (from natural gas or naphtha)	Fibers
Isoprene	Isoamylene (from refinery liquids) or propylene (see above) or by-product from cracking naphtha	Rubbers
Synthetic methanol	Natural gas or naphtha	Fibers, plastics, and resins
Orthoxylene	Refinery reformate (from naphtha)	Fibers and plastics
Synthetic phenol	Benzene (see above) and propylene (see above)	Plastics
Paraxylene	Refinery reformate (from naphtha)	Fibers
Styrene monomer	Benzene (see above) and ethylene (see propylene above)	Plastics and rubbers
Vinyl chloride monomer	Ethylene (see above) and chlorine (from salt and electricity)	Plastics

Example of Decline in Oligopolistic Profits with Increased Competition

The results of this study indicate that from the years 1960 to 1962 until 1963 to 1965, the number of producers of styrene monomer increased from eight to ten, and the estimated oligopolistic profit declined from 1.8¢ per pound to 0.3¢ per pound. The study relied on a number of assumptions. Any changes in the assumptions might affect the estimation of the *level* of oligopoly profit and might even affect the estimation of a *change in the level* of oligopoly profit. It seems doubtful, however, that any reasonable changes in assumptions would affect the *direction* of change; therefore, one is left with the conclusion that almost surely the level of oligopolistic profit in styrene monomer manufacture dropped from the 1960–1962 period to that of 1963–1965.

The following table, which was based on published information, presents the details.

	Period	
Item	*1960–1962*	*1963–1965*
Basic Data		
Number of producers[a]	8	10
Average annual production, total U.S. (millions of pounds)	1,816	2,530
Average annual production per producer (millions of pounds)	227	253
Change in average production per producer (percent)	—	+11%

Change in capital-related costs per unit of output due to increased production[b]	—	−4%
Change in labor costs per unit of output due to increased production[c]	—	−8%
Change in unit costs of all items,[d] except benzene and ethylene (see below)	—	+4%

Calculated Unit Value[e]	(All numbers in cents per pound of styrene monomer)	
Benzene[f]	3.5	2.8
Ethylene[g]	1.6	1.5
Other raw materials and utilities[h]	1.0	1.0
Subtotal, raw materials and utilities	6.1	5.3
Labor and supervision[i]	0.2	0.2
Maintenance, taxes, and miscellaneous capital-related costs[j]	0.3	0.3
Depreciation and return on investment[k]	1.8	1.7
Sales and administrative expense[l]	0.5	0.5
Correction in value added because of additional operating experience between 1960–1962 and 1963–1965[m]	0.3	—
Total value added	3.1	2.7
Total sales value required for "competitive price"	9.2	8.0
Actual sales value[n]	11.0	8.3
Estimated "oligopoly profit"	1.8	0.3

[a] Concentration ratio, measured as percentage of production of four largest producers also was declining, from 82 in 1959 to 68 in 1966.

[b] Plant factor = 0.6 in the equation $C_2 = C_1 (S_2/S_1)^a$, where C_1 = construction cost of plant No. 1; C_2 = construction cost of plant No. 2; S_1 = capacity of plant No. 1; S_2 = capacity of plant No. 2; and a = plant factor.

[c] Plant factor = 0.2; see note b, above.

[d] Assumed to be equal to change in GNP deflator. See U.S. Department of Commerce, Office of Business Economics, *Survey of Current Business*, August 1965, July 1966, and April 1967.

[e] Estimates for the period 1963–1965 calculated from data in Robert B. Stobaugh, *Petrochemical Manufacturing and Marketing Guide*, vol. 1 (Houston: Gulf Publishing Company, 1968), p. 88; and Claude Mercier, *Petrochemical Industry and the Possibilities of Its Establishment in the Developing Countries* (Paris: Editions Technip, 1966), p. 124. Estimates for the period 1960–1962 derived by ratio from 1963–1965 estimates through factors as noted.

^f Unit value of benzene = 29¢ a gallon in the period 1960–1962 and 23¢ in the years 1963–1965. U.S. Tariff Commission, *Synthetic Organic Chemicals: U.S. Production and Sales* (Washington, DC: GPO), various years. Yield of styrene from benzene estimated to be unchanged.

^g Unit value of ethylene = 4.9¢ a pound in the years 1960–1962 and 4.5¢ during 1963–1965. U.S. Tariff Commission, *Synthetic Organic Chemicals: U.S. Production and Sales,* various years. Yield of styrene from ethylene estimated to be unchanged.

^h Estimated to have increased between the periods 1960–1962 and 1963–1965 by same amount as GNP deflator.

ⁱ Estimated to have decreased by 8 percent between the periods 1960–1962 and 1963–1965 because of increased production and increased by 4 percent because of change in unit costs of labor.

^j Estimated that between the periods 1960–1962 and 1963–1965 changes in cost as a result of increased production were offset by changes in unit costs of inputs.

^k Estimated to have decreased by 8 percent between the periods 1960–1962 and 1963–1965 because of increased production.

^l Estimated that there was no change between the periods 1960–1962 and 1963–1965.

^m Calculated on assumption that a doubling of cumulative production resulted in a drop of 20 percent in value added. In this case, the cumulative U.S. production was 44 percent greater at the midpoint of production in the years 1963–1965 compared with the years 1960–1962; therefore, calculations indicate a value added per unit in the period 1962–1965 of 89 percent of that in the 1960–1962 period—a relationship attributable solely to the experience effect. This correction factor was added to estimated 1960–1962 costs since the basic data from which these costs were obtained were for the 1963–1965 period (see note e, above).

ⁿ U.S. Tariff Commission, *Synthetic Organic Chemicals: U.S. Production and Sales,* various years.

NOTES

CHAPTER I

1. Joseph A. Schumpeter, *Capitalism, Socialism and Democracy* (New York: Harper & Row, 1976. Originally published in 1942), chapter VII, "The Process of Creative Destruction." Also see, Joseph A. Schumpeter, *The Theory of Economic Development* (Cambridge, MA: Harvard University Press, 1961. Originally published in 1934), chapter IV, "Entrepreneurial Profit."

2. This definition is from Michael E. Porter, "Competition in Global Industries: A Conceptual Framework," in Michael E. Porter, ed., *Competition in Global Industries* (Boston: Harvard Business School Press, 1986), p. 18.

3. The references in this note and notes 4, 5, and 6, below, are intended to be illustrative rather than exhaustive.
   For examples of this approach, see Theodore Levitt, "Exploit the Product Life Cycle," *Harvard Business Review,* November–December 1965, pp. 81–94. See also Donald K. Clifford, Jr., "Managing the Product Life-Cycle," *European Business,* July 1969, pp. 7–15; and William E. Cox, Jr., "Product Life Cycles as Marketing Models," *Journal of Business,* October 1967, pp. 373–384. For a summary of empirical tests of the concept, see Rolando Polli and Victor Cook, "Validity of the Product Life Cycle," *The Journal of Business,* October 1969, pp. 385–400.

4. For example, see Michael E. Porter, *Competitive Strategy: Techniques for Analyzing Industries and Competitors* (New York: Free Press, 1980).

5. For examples, see W. J. Abernathy and P. L. Townsend, "Technology, Productivity and Process Change," *Technological Forecasting and Social Change,* vol. 7, no. 4, 1975; William J. Abernathy and James M. Utterback, "Patterns of Industrial Innovation," *Technology Review,* June/July 1978; and W. J. Abernathy, K. Clark, and A. Kantrow, *Industrial Renaissance* (New York: Basic Books, 1983).

6. For examples of analyses emphasizing marketing factors, see Raymond Vernon, "International Investment and International Trade in the Product Cycle," *Quarterly Journal of Economics,* May 1966, pp. 190–207; Louis T. Wells, Jr., *The Product Life Cycle and International Trade* (Boston: Harvard Business School Division of Research, 1972); and Raymond Vernon, "The Product Cycle Hypothesis in a New International Environment," *Oxford Bulletin,* November 1979, pp. 255–267.

For examples of related analyses emphasizing technology, see M. V. Posner, "International Trade and Technological Change," *Oxford Economic Papers*, XIII, October 1961, pp. 323–341; and G. C. Hufbauer, *Synthetic Materials and the Theory of International Trade* (Cambridge, MA: Harvard University Press, 1966).

For a discussion of changes over time for an industry (rather than a product), see my "How Investment Abroad Creates Jobs at Home," *Harvard Business Review*, September–October 1972, pp. 118–126.

7. Because most governments ordinarily collect statistics for chemicals rather than petrochemicals, any estimate of petrochemical output is approximate and depends on the exact categories of chemicals an analyst includes in the totals. As mentioned in chapter 1, I used the same categories as did the U.S. Department of Commerce (see Appendix B). I made these estimates after reviewing internal documents at Arthur D. Little, Inc., interviewing a specialist at the U.S. Department of Commerce, and studying the following sources: U.S. Department of Commerce, *U.S. Industrial Outlook, 1986* (Washington, DC: GPO, 1986), p. 11-2; U.S. Department of Commerce, *A Competitive Assessment of the U.S. Petrochemical Industry* (Washington, DC: August 31, 1982); United States International Trade Commission, *The Shift from U.S. Production of Commodity Petrochemicals to Value-Added Specialty Chemical Products and the Possible Impact on U.S. Trade,* USITC Publication 1677 (Washington, DC: April 1985); Organization for Economic Cooperation and Development [OECD], *Petrochemical Industry: Energy Aspects of Structural Change* (Paris: OECD, 1985); UNIDO Secretariat, *World Changes in the Structure of the Petrochemical Industry 1980–1983* (Vienna: United Nations Industrial Development Organization, October 9, 1985); UNIDO Secretariat, *Current World Situation in Petrochemicals* (Vienna: United Nations Industrial Development Organization, November 14, 1985); *Chemical Week,* January 28, 1987, pp. 20–30; Data Resources Incorporated, *World Plastics Review,* Winter 1987; and *The Economist,* May 16, 1987, pp. 76–77.

8. The official name of West Germany, of course, is the Federal Republic of Germany, but I use West Germany because that term is most often used by executives in the petrochemical industry. For data supporting this paragraph, see U.S. Department of Commerce, Bureau of the Census, *U.S. Imports for Consumption and General Imports,* FT246/Annual (Washington, DC: GPO), various years; U.S. Department of Commerce, Bureau of the Census, *U.S. Exports Schedule B Commodity by Country,* FT446/Annual (Washington, DC: GPO), various years; U.S. Department of Commerce, *Survey of Current Business,* monthly (Washington, DC: GPO), various issues; *Chemical Week,* September 11, 1985, pp. 22–25; and *The Economist,* May 2, 1987, p. 23.

9. A list of 12 "footloose" manufactured chemical products appeared in a booklet published by Monsanto Company (*Facts about Monsanto and the Hydrocarbon Division,* not dated, but published about 1964). From this list, 2 products were deleted because freight costs for transportation between continents were so high relative to the value of the product that international trade had been negligible, and 1 was deleted because adequate data could not be obtained on world production facilities. I authored or coauthored an article about each of the nine products (plus some other products) in *Hydrocarbon Processing* between 1965 and 1973. There were a total of 20 articles in this series. Fourteen of the 20 articles were subsequently published in my *Petrochemical Manufacturing and Marketing Guide,* vol. 1, *Aromatics and Derivatives* (Houston: Gulf Publishing, 1966) and *Petrochemical Manufacturing and Marketing Guide,* vol. 2, *Olefins, Diolefins, and Acetylene* (Houston: Gulf Publishing, 1968).

10. My estimates from U.S. International Trade Commission, *Synthetic Organic Chemicals—U.S. Production and Sales* (Washington, DC: GPO), annual; U.S. Department of Commerce, Bureau of the Census, *U.S. Imports for Consumption and General Im-*

ports, FT246/Annual (Washington, DC: GPO), various years; U.S. Department of Commerce, Bureau of the Census, *U.S. Exports Schedule B Commodity by Country,* FT446/Annual (Washington, DC: GPO), various years; Chemical Intelligence Service files; and unpublished documents of Arthur D. Little, Inc.

11. *CPI Purchasing,* March 1985, p. 33.

CHAPTER 2

1. The definition of product innovation was adapted from Edwin Mansfield et al., *Research and Innovation in the Modern Corporation* (New York: W. W. Norton, 1971), chap. 6, who refer to both new products and new processes as "innovations." Also see Edwin Mansfield and John Rapoport, "The Costs of Industrial Product Innovations," *Management Sciences,* August 1975, pp. 1380–1381; and Donald G. Marquis, "The Anatomy of Successful Innovations," *Innovation,* no. 7, 1969, p. 28. Other authors refer to a commercial development as an "innovation" only if it results in a new product; see OECD, *Plastics: Gaps in Technology* (Paris: 1969), p. 17. Profit estimates from author's interviews with industry executives. The $450,000 excluded some general purpose equipment used to make a variety of resins, including the one in question.

2. Edwin Mansfield et al., *Research and Innovation in the Modern Corporation,* chap. 2; and Edwin Mansfield and John Rapoport, "The Costs of Industrial Product Innovations," *Management Science,* August 1975, pp. 1380–1386.
   Studies of returns to R&D expenditures often have one or more of the following limitations: estimates are for the social rather than the private rate of return; estimates are for all industries rather than just chemicals; when estimates are for chemicals, they almost never are given for the petrochemical sector. In addition, the authors usually state certain qualifications about the data. With these limitations in mind, it appears that returns on chemical R&D are higher than the average for industry and that social rates are higher than private rates. Estimates for the private rate of return for chemical R&D range from about 10 percent to 90 percent. For a summary of results, see Edwin Mansfield, "Microeconomics of Technological Innovation," in Ralph Landau and Nathan Rosenberg, eds., *The Positive Sum Strategy* (Washington, DC: National Academy Press, 1986), pp. 308–311. For estimates of private returns to chemical R&D, see Zvi Griliches, "Returns to Research and Development Expenditures in the Private Sector," in J. Kendrick and B. Vaccara, eds., *New Developments in Productivity Measurement and Analysis* (Chicago: University of Chicago Press, 1980). For estimates of private and social returns to chemical R&D on three innovations, see Edwin Mansfield et al., "Social and Private Rates of Return from Industrial Innovations," *Quarterly Journal of Economics,* May 1977, pp. 221–240; and *The Production and Application of New Industrial Technology* (New York: W. W. Norton, 1977). For estimates of social returns to chemical R&D, see Edwin Mansfield, "Rates of Return from Industrial Research and Development," *American Economic Review,* May 1965, pp. 310–322, and J. Minasian, "Research and Development, Product Functions, and Rates of Return," *American Economic Review,* May 1969, pp. 80–85. For estimates of social and private returns for industry in general, see Foster Associates, *A Survey on Net Rates of Return on Innovations* (Washington, DC: National Science Foundation, 1978), and Robert R. Nathan Associates, *Net Rates of Return on Innovations* (Washington, DC: National Science Foundation, 1978). For recent estimates of private returns for industry in general, see Kim B. Clark and Zvi Griliches, "Productivity Growth and R&D at the Business Level," in Zvi Griliches, ed., *R&D, Patents, and Productivity* (Chicago: University of Chicago Press, 1984), chap. 19.

3. For further discussion of the use of outside sources of knowledge, see Richard S. Rosenbloom, "Product Innovation in a Scientific Age," *New Ideas for Successful Marketing* (Chicago: Proceedings of the 1986 World Congress, American Marketing Association, 1966), chap. 23; and Raymond Vernon, "Location of Economic Activity," in John H. Dunning, ed., *Economic Analysis and the Multinational Enterprise* (London: George Allen & Unwin, 1974). For a study of an earlier time period that shows that Du Pont relied on inventions made outside the firm for the basic knowledge in 10 of 13 commercially significant products, see Willard F. Mueller, "The Origins of the Basic Inventions Underlying Du Pont's Major Product and Process Innovations, 1920–1950," *The Rate and Direction of Inventive Activity* (Princeton: Princeton University Press, 1962), p. 343; National Science Foundation, *Trends to 1982 in Industrial Support of Basic Research,* Special Report NSF 83-302 (Washington, DC: National Science Foundation, 1983). The low level of spending on basic research is typical for most industries because of the spillover of results outside the firm's boundaries. For levels of research expenditures, see Keith Pavitt, *The Conditions for Success in Technological Innovation* (Paris: OECD, 1971), pp. 79–103; and *Chemical & Engineering News,* July 28, 1986, pp. 32–60. There is evidence, however, that for industry in general, the increase of total factor productivity of a firm is related positively to the amount of basic research it carries out; see Edwin Mansfield, "Microeconomics of Technological Innovation," in Landau and Rosenberg, eds., *The Positive Sum Strategy,* p. 311.

4. For a more thorough discussion, see Therese Flaherty, "Information as a National Economic Resource," *Conference Proceedings,* The International Congress on Applied Systems Research and Cybernetics, 1981 (available in mimeograph from Associate Professor Therese Flaherty, Harvard Business School).

5. These contacts were traced from historical sources in notes 6 and 8, below.

6. This history of styrene is from A. J. Warner, "Introduction," and R. H. Boundy and Sylvia M. Stoesser, "History," in Ray H. Boundy, Raymond F. Boyer, and Sylvia M. Stoesser, eds., *Styrene: Its Polymer, Co-polymers, and Derivatives* (New York: Reinhold, 1952), pp. 1–12; Ernst von Meyer, *A History of Physical Chemistry* (London: Macmillan, 1960), p. 542; W. C. Teach and A. C. Kiessling, *Polystyrene* (New York: Reinhold, 1960), pp. 1–7; and Raymond E. Kirk and Donald F. Othmer, *Encyclopedia of Chemical Technology* (New York: Wiley, 1947–56, 1978).

7. It is my impression that product patents are less important in providing monopoly protection for commercializers of relatively simple molecules, such as styrene monomer, than for commercializers of complicated petrochemicals, such as polymers, elastomers, and fibers. Product patents are also important in certain nonpetrochemical sectors of the chemical industry in which the molecules are very complex; for evidence on pharmaceuticals, see Eric von Hippel, "Appropriability of Innovation Benefit as a Predictor of the Source of Innovation," *Research Policy,* April 1982, pp. 95–115.

It is my impression that process patents are quite important in the petrochemical industry. Overall, for a given level of R&D, the chemical industry's propensity to patent is significantly higher than the average for U.S. manufacturing industry, see John Bound et al., "Who Does R&D and Who Patents?" in Zvi Griliches, ed., *R&D, Patents, and Productivity,* chap. 2. In the chemical and pharmaceutical industries, patent protection was judged by the firms selected in a random sample to have been essential for 30 percent or more of the innovations and over 80 percent of the patentable inventions reported to have been patented; see Edwin Mansfield, "Microeconomics of Technological Change," pp. 315–316. See also Richard C. Levin, Alvin K. Klevorick, Richard R. Nelson, and Sidney G. Winter, "Survey Research on R&D Appropriability and Technological Opportunity: Part I," Working Paper, Yale University, July 1984. One study found that process patent activity was positively related to "learning by doing" (for more about this see chapter 5) and market size; see Marvin B.

Lieberman, "Patents, Learning by Doing, and Market Structure in the Chemical Processing Industries," *International Journal of Industrial Organization* (forthcoming).

8. The historical information in the following six paragraphs of the text was taken from Raymond E. Kirk and Donald F. Othmer, *Encyclopedia of Chemical Technology;* Georg Lockenmann, *The Story of Chemistry* (New York: Philosophical Library, 1959), pp. 202–203, 257–258; D. W. F. Hardie and J. Davidson Pratt, *A History of the Modern British Chemical Industry* (Oxford: Pergamon Press, 1966), pp. 62–63; Alexander Findley, *A Hundred Years of Chemistry* (New York: Macmillan, 1937), p. 156; Ernst von Meyer, *A History of Chemistry* (New York: Macmillan, 1891), p. 404; Henry M. Leicester, *The Historical Background of Chemistry* (New York: Wiley, 1956), pp. 176–177; Edward Farber, ed., *Great Chemists* (New York: Interscience Publishers, 1961), pp. 735–747, 1147–1156; *Modern Plastics Encyclopedia,* vol. 1 (New York: Plastics Catalog Corporation, 1947), p. 147; J. H. DuBois, *Plastics* (Chicago: American Technical Society, 1943), p. 298; W. J. S. Nannton, *Synthetic Rubber* (London: Macmillan, 1937), pp. 3–13, 37; Aaron J. Ihde, *The Development of Modern Chemistry* (New York: Harper & Row, 1964), p. 630; F. Sherwood Taylor, *A History of Industrial Chemistry* (London: Heinemann, 1957), pp. 230–238, 433; and Wilhelm Rossersdorf, *In the Realm of Chemistry* (Düsseldorf: Econ-Verlag, 1965).

9. For examples of debottlenecking, see Samuel Hollander, *The Sources of Increased Efficiency: A Study of Du Pont Rayon Plastics* (Cambridge, MA: MIT Press, 1965). For a discussion of adding capacity to prevent entry of other firms, see chapter 5.

10. Economists have spelled out conditions under which contracting of open-market sales can substitute for intracompany transfers, but the very imperfect markets that exist early in the commercial life of a product are unlikely to enable open-market sales to be good substitutes for intracompany transfers. See Oliver Williamson, *Markets and Hierarchies* (New York: Free Press, 1975), and "The Modern Corporation: Origins, Evolution, Attributes," *Journal of Economic Literature,* December 1981, pp. 1537–1568; also see chapter 6, note 6, below. In any case, executives in the petrochemical industry usually do not consider intercompany sales to be the equivalent of intracompany transfers. This remark by an executive is typical: "If the monomer manufacturer can develop captive polymer uses and capacity, he insulates himself (to an extent) from the commercial exigencies of the merchant monomer market. Among other things, he may be able to increase his scale of manufacture sooner than his merchant competitor, or ride out down swings in certain market sectors. Thus captive use is another effective 'weapon' in the petrochemical arsenal." Private correspondence, July 1986.

11. A study of 48 products in 4 industries, of which one was chemicals, indicates that, on average, an imitating firm can imitate a new product in about two-thirds the time and at two-thirds the cost expended by the innovator, and that patent protection by the innovator increases the imitator's cost by about 10 percent in chemicals. See Edwin Mansfield, "Microeconomics of Technological Change," pp. 312–314.

12. Foster Grant's technology employed the same basic principles as did Dow's and Monsanto's, but Foster Grant's smaller plant made it less efficient. See my *Petrochemical Manufacturing and Marketing Guide,* vol. 1, *Aromatics and Derivatives* (Houston: Gulf Publishing, pp. 72, 87–89; and Raymond E. Kirk and Donald F. Othmer, *Encyclopedia of Chemical Technology.* Date of Foster Grant start-up: letter from company.

13. W. J. Abernathy, K. Clark, and A. Kantrow use the term *epochal* to describe what I have called a major innovation; see their *Industrial Renaissance* (New York: Basic Books, 1983).

14. Robert B. Stobaugh, *Petrochemical Manufacturing and Marketing Guide,* vol. 1, *Aromatics and Derivatives,* chap. 6, "Phenol."

15. See note 2, above.

16. In addition to these reasons, there could be some unknown product-specific factors at work in the case of the nine products; for as shown in Figure 2-1, all nine products were not represented in all decades.

17. On increase and then decrease in process innovation, see William J. Abernathy and Phillip L. Townsend, "Technology, Productivity and Process Change," *Technological Forecasting and Social Change,* vol. 7, No. 4, 1975, pp. 388–393; William J. Abernathy and James M. Utterback, "Patterns of Industrial Innovation," *Technology Review,* June/July 1978, p. 40; and Richard Foster, *Innovation: The Attacker's Advantage* (New York: Summit Books, 1986), pp. 32–35, 116–129.

18. The probability (p) that the next process developed for any one of the nine products would represent a major innovation, where X_1 was the number of previous innovations for that product was $\log_e [p/(1-p)] = .22 - .95 \log_e X_1$.

19. *Chemical Week,* December 7, 1968, p. 56. Also letter to author from Arco Chemical, June 3, 1974.

20. Richard R. Nelson and Sidney G. Winter, "In Search of a Useful Theory of Innovation," *Research Policy,* January 1977, p. 45. For evidence that the technological environments of some industries, including chemicals, offer greater opportunities for product innovation than the technological environments of other industries, see Robert W. Wilson, "The Effect of Technological Environment and Product Rivalry on R&D Effort and Licensing of Inventions," *The Review of Economics and Statistics,* May 1977, pp. 171–178. For other research that stresses technological opportunity as a motivator of R&D, see Richard C. Levin and Peter C. Reiss, "Tests of a Schumpeteran Model of R&D and Market Structure," Ariel Pakes and Mark Schankerman, "An Exploration into the Determinants of Research Intensity," and Kim B. Clark and Zvi Griliches, "Productivity Growth and R&D at the Business Level," in Zvi Griliches, ed., *R&D, Patents, and Productivity,* chaps. 8, 9, and 19; and Richard C. Levin, Wesley M. Cohen, and David C. Mowery, "R&D, Appropriability, Opportunity, and Market Structure: New Evidence on Some Schumpeterian Hypotheses," *Issues in the Economics of R&D,* May 1985, pp. 20–24.

21. This conclusion is consistent with the statement that "technological inputs have the least impact where they are needed most, in mature, or stagnant industries": Abernathy and Townsend, "Technology Productivity and Process Change," p. 381. As mentioned earlier, a drop in monolopy rents in addition to a decline in technological opportunities could be a factor in the decline in innovation.

CHAPTER 3

1. This conclusion about typicalness is based on discussions with industry reviewers of this book, plus my experience with the industry, during which I have been involved directly or indirectly with dozens of attempts at innovation.

2. Alpha estimates are taken from company records and interviews with an Alpha engineer, estimates on the polymer commercialization from records of the other company referred to.

3. For a description of this function, see Paul Lawrence and Jay Lorsch, *Organization and Environment* (Boston: Harvard Business School Division of Research, 1967); and André Reudi and P. Lawrence, "Organizations in Two Cultures," in P. Lawrence and J. Lorsch, *Studies in Organization* (Homewood, IL: Richard D. Irwin, 1970). The latter describes the difference in approaches to this role in the German and U.S. cultures.

4. The classic formulation of the two extreme types of uncertainty into uncertainty and risk was made by Frank Knight, *Risk, Uncertainty and Profit* (Chicago: University of Chicago Press, 1971 [originally published Boston: Houghton Mifflin, 1921]), chap. 7. For a discussion by Bayesian statisticians, see Robert Schlaifer and Arthur Schleifer, Jr., "Introduction to Data Analysis" (Boston: Harvard Business School, 1985, mimeograph), p. 44. The search for knowledge by conducting R&D activity is similar in concept to the search for the lowest price when the distribution of prices is unknown; for a discussion of the latter, see Michael Rothschild, "Searching for the Lowest Price When the Distribution of Price Is Unknown," *Journal of Political Economy,* July/August 1974, pp. 689–711. For the use of the word *uncertainty* in innovation literature, refer to William Abernathy and James Utterback, "Patterns of Industrial Innovation," *Technology Review,* June/July 1978, p. 45; and Richard R. Nelson and Sidney G. Winter, "In Search of a Useful Theory of Innovation," *Research Policy,* January 1977, pp. 47, 71.

5. This two-category classification is discussed in Abernathy and Utterback, "Patterns of Industrial Innovation," pp. 41–47.

6. Richard S. Rosenbloom, "Product Innovation in a Scientific Age," *New Ideas for Successful Marketing* (Chicago: Proceedings of the 1966 World Congress, American Marketing Association, 1966), chap. 23; and Raymond Vernon, "Location of Economic Activity," in John H. Dunning, ed., *Economic Analysis and the Multinational Enterprise* (London: George Allen & Unwin, 1974). Close integration among R&D, marketing, and economic evaluators increases the probability of commercialization; see Edwin Mansfield and Samuel Wagner, "Organizational and Strategic Factors Associated with Probabilities of Success in Industrial R&D," *Journal of Business,* April 1975, pp. 179–198. Also, see Paul Lawrence and Jay Lorsch, *Organization and Environment.*

7. W. Carl Kester, "Today's Options for Tomorrow's Growth," *Harvard Business Review,* March–April 1984, pp. 153–160.

8. These steps are adapted from Booz, Allen & Hamilton, Inc., *New Products Management for the 1980s* (New York, 1982), pp. 3, 11. Other authors use somewhat different steps: for example, scientific discovery, invention, development, innovation (commercialization), and diffusion (broad application); see William J. Abernathy and Phillip L. Townsend, "Technology, Productivity and Process Change," *Technological Forecasting and Social Change,* vol. 7, No. 4, 1975, pp. 380–381, who state that the linear model "is certainly valid in the sense that events do occur in the suggested sequence," although they do caution that it "is more misleading than useful." For still other expositions of a linear model, see S. Meyers and D. Marquis, *Successful Industrial Innovations,* Report No. 69–17 (Washington, DC: National Science Foundation, 1969); Kevin Roberts and Martin L. Weitzman, "Funding Criteria for Research, Development, and Exploration Projects," *Econometrica,* September 1981, pp. 1261–1288; and Richard S. Rosenbloom, "Managing Technology for the Longer Term: A Managerial Perspective" and Ken-ichi Imai, Ikujiro Nonaka, and Hirotaka Takeuchi, "Managing the New Product Development Process: How Japanese Companies Learn and Unlearn," in Kim B. Clark, Robert H. Hayes, and Christopher Lorenz, eds., *The Uneasy Alliance: Managing the Productivity-Technology Dilemma* (Boston: Harvard

Business School Press, 1985), chaps. 7 and 8. The last reference includes a discussion of the advantages of some simultaneity in stages (p. 350).

9. For a discussion of "demand pull" and "technology push" see C. Freeman, *The Economics of Industrial Innovation*, 2d ed. (Cambridge, MA: MIT Press, 1982), pp. 109–111; Keith Pavitt, *The Conditions for Success in Technological Innovation* (Paris: OECD, 1971), pp. 52–55; and Richard S. Rosenbloom, "Product Innovation in a Scientific Age." The backing-and-forthing pattern is hypothesized in Richard B. Nelson and Sidney G. Winter, p. 55.

10. This argument is found in Nelson and Winter, "In Search of a Useful Theory of Innovation," pp. 51–53.

11. Ibid., pp. 44, 65.

12. See chapter 6, below, for data on process developments by petrochemical manufacturers compared with engineering firms.

13. Abernathy and Utterback, "Patterns of Industrial Innovation," p. 45.

14. The importance of suppliers of goods is emphasized in Max Hall, ed., *Made in New York* (Cambridge, MA: Harvard University Press, 1959), Nathan Rosenberg, *Inside the Black Box: Technology and Economics* (Cambridge: Cambridge University Press, 1982), chap. 3, and is implicit in the "uncoordinated" and the "fluid" stages described in Abernathy and Townsend, "Technology, Productivity and Process Change," p. 390, and Abernathy and Utterback, "Patterns of Industrial Innovation," pp. 40–42. Certain case studies of innovation have highlighted the importance of the market, but typically the extent of contact with the market is not documented; for an example, see Leonard S. Reich, "Industrial Research and the Pursuit of Corporate Security: The Early Years of Bell Labs," *Business History Review*, Winter 1980, pp. 504–529. The importance of the market is also emphasized in Hall, *Made in New York*, and a long line of research flowing from that work. See Raymond Vernon, "International Investment and International Trade in the Product Cycle," *Quarterly Journal of Economics*, May 1966, pp. 109–207, and *Sovereignty at Bay* (New York: Basic Books, 1971), and Louis T. Wells, Jr., ed., *The Product Life Cycle and International Trade* (Boston: Harvard Business School Division of Research, 1972). For a separate line of research that reaches similar conclusions about the importance of the market, see N. R. Baker et al., "The Effects of Perceived Needs and Means on the Generation of Ideas for Industrial R&D Projects," *IEEE Trans. Eng. Management*, December 1967, pp. 156–163; Meyers and Marquis, *Successful Industrial Innovations;* and Abernathy and Townsend, "Technology, Productivity and Process Change"—although the latter study contains an interesting twist in pointing out that one firm's *product* innovation often represents a *process* innovation for the target market.

CHAPTER 4

1. See note 2, chapter 2, above.

2. Raymond Vernon, *Sovereignty at Bay* (New York: Basic Books, 1971), chap. 3.

3. William Abernathy and James Utterback, "Patterns of Industrial Innovation," *Technology Review*, June/July 1978, p. 42.

4. Vernon, *Sovereignty at Bay*, and G. C. Hufbauer, *Synthetic Materials and the Theory of International Trade* (Cambridge, MA: Harvard University Press, 1960).

5. Raymond Vernon, *Metropolis 1985* (Cambridge, MA: Harvard University Press, 1960), chaps. 2 and 6, and Robert Lichtenberg, *One-Tenth of a Nation* (Cambridge, MA: Harvard University Press, 1960), p. 18 and chap. 2.

6. David Teece, "Technology Transfer by Multinational Firms: The Resource Cost of Transferring Technological Know How," *Economic Journal*, June 1977, pp. 242–261.

7. H. M. Corley, ed., *Successful Commercial Chemical Development* (New York: Wiley, 1954), pp. 142, 347.

8. Roger Williams, Jr., "Why Cost Estimates Go Astray," *Chemical Engineering Progress*, April 1964, p. 18.

9. Robert B. Stobaugh et al., *Nine Investments Abroad and Their Impact at Home* (Boston: Harvard Business School Division of Research, 1976). This preference slackens as firms gain more experience abroad, however; see Raymond Vernon and William H. Davidson, "Foreign Production of Technology-intensive Products by U.S.-based Multinational Enterprises," a study funded by the National Science Foundation (Boston: January 1979, mimeograph).

10. See *Plastics: Gaps in Technology* (Paris: OECD, 1969), p. 97; and Gary C. Hufbauer, *Synthetic Materials and the Theory of International Trade* (Cambridge, MA: Harvard University Press, 1966).

11. "World-Wide HPI Construction Boxscore," *Hydrocarbon Processing*, February 1977, Section 2.

12. See a brief description and references in Dennis C. Mueller and John E. Tilton, "Research and Development Costs as a Barrier to Entry," *Canadian Journal of Economics*, November 1969, pp. 570–579. See also, Edwin Mansfield, "Size of Firm, Market Structure, and Innovation," *Journal of Political Economy*, December 1963, p. 556; F. M. Scherer, *Industrial Market Structure and Economic Performance*, 2d ed. (Chicago: Rand-McNally, 1980), pp. 413–418; and A. Cooper, "R and D Is More Efficient in Small Companies," *Harvard Business Review*, June 1969, pp. 75–83. More recent research indicates that the elasticity of R&D with respect to sales is close to unity for 19 of the 21 U.S. manufacturing industries, including chemicals; the exceptions are the textile industry and miscellaneous manufacturing; see John Bond et al., "Who Does R&D and Who Patents?" in Zvi Griliches, ed., *R&D, Patents, and Productivity* (Chicago: University of Chicago Press, 1984), chap. 2. Also see Wesley M. Cohen, Richard C. Levin, and David C. Mowery, "Firm Size and R&D Intensity: A Re-Examination," *Journal of Industrial Economics*, June 1987.

13. See Raymond Vernon, "Organization as a Scale Factor in the Growth of Firms," in Jesse Markham and Gus Papanek, *Industrial Organization and Economic Development* (Boston: Houghton Mifflin, 1970), and Raymond Vernon, *Storm over the Multinationals* (Cambridge, MA: Harvard University Press, 1977), chap. 3. Vernon has an excellent bibliography, which I will not repeat here.

14. Vernon, "Organization as a Scale Factor in the Growth of Firms."

15. B. David Halpern, "Growth Problems of a Small R&D-Oriented Specialty Company," in E. Balgley, P. S. Gilchrist, and P. B. Slawter, *The Small Chemical Enterprise and Forces Shaping the Future of the Chemical Industry* (New York: Chemical Marketing and Economics Division, American Chemical Society, 1973), p. 43. I have seen this factor operate first hand in my consulting work with product innovators. Also see E. K. Bolton, "Development of Nylon," *Chemtech*, July 1976, p. 463; and Rowland T. Moriarty, *Industrial Buying Behavior* (Lexington, MA: Lexington Books, 1983).

16. See chapter 6 below. Also see W. W. Alberts and S. H. Archer, "Some Evidence on the Effect of Company Size on the Cost of Equity Capital," *Journal of Financial and Quantitative Analysis,* March 1973, pp. 229–242.

17. See P. J. Buckley and M. Casson, *The Future of the Multinational Enterprise* (New York: Holmes and Meier, 1976), chap. 2.

18. See Raymond Vernon, "Location of Economic Activity," in John H. Dunning, ed., *Economic Analysis and the Multinational Enterprise* (London: George Allen & Unwin, 1974); Vernon, "Organization as a Scale Factor in the Growth of Firms"; Thomas J. Allen, *Managing the Flow of Technology* (Cambridge, MA: MIT Press, 1977); Richard S. Rosenbloom and F. W. Wolek, *Technology, Information and Organization* (Boston: Harvard Business School Division of Research, 1967).

19. For the idea that diversification is advantageous in making use of research results, see Richard R. Nelson, "The Simple Economics of Basic Scientific Research," *Journal of Political Economy,* June 1959, pp. 297–306. The following studies show a correlation between diversification and R&D intensity: André Lemelin, "Relatedness in the Patterns of Interindustry Diversification," *Review of Economics and Statistics,* November 1982, pp. 650–651; and James M. MacDonald, "R&D and the Directions of Diversification," *Review of Economics and Statistics,* November 1985, pp. 583–590.

20. In a survey of 13,000 new products introduced between 1976 and 1981 by 700 large U.S. manufacturers, a 71 percent experience curve was found; that is, with each doubling of the number of new products introduced by a company, the cost of each introduction declined by 29 percent; see Booz, Allen & Hamilton, Inc., *New Products Management for the 1980s* (New York, 1982), p. 18. Also see Jean-Paul Sallenave, *Experience Analysis for Industrial Planning* (Lexington, MA: Lexington Books, 1976).

21. See note 12, above.

22. See Edwin Mansfield, *Industrial Research and Technological Innovation* (New York: W. W. Norton, 1968), p. 42, for evidence that in the chemical industry there are scale economies in R&D activities (increases in R&D expenditures are associated with more than proportional increases in inventive output, when the effect of firm size is held constant by statistical methods), but when R&D expenditures are held constant, the size of firm is associated with decreases in inventive output. In contrast, another study found no statistically significant relationship between firm size and R&D inputs in those industrial chemical firms that perform R&D; see William S. Comanor, "Market Structure, Product Differentiation, and Industrial Research," *Quarterly Journal of Economics,* November 1967, p. 641. Still another study found that R&D intensity increased with firm size in the chemical industry; see F. M. Scherer, "Size of Firm, Oligopoly, and Research: A Comment," *Canadian Journal of Economics,* May 1965, pp. 256–266. But, as mentioned in note 12, above, more recent research indicates that the elasticity of R&D with respect to sales is close to unity for chemicals; see John Bond et al., "Who Does R&D and Who Patents?" in Zvi Griliches, ed., *R&D, Patents, and Productivity,* chap. 2.

23. *Plastics: Gaps in Technology,* p. 97.

24. Such results are consistent with the argument of Mueller and Tilton, "Research and Development Costs as a Barrier to Entry," except that stages in development apply to a whole industry rather than a product.

25. The importance of large size in product innovation is supported also by a historical description of the commercialization of organophosphorus insecticides, which are pet-rochemical compounds made from phosphorus and organic chemicals. See Batelle Columbus Laboratories, *Interaction of Science and Technology in the Innovative Process: Some Case Studies,* Report for NSF under Contract NSF-C-667, March 19, 1973, chap. 9.

The relationship between firm size and product innovation in other industries is less certain than in petrochemicals. The principal product innovators were large firms in videocassette recorders, both large and small firms in semiconductors, and small firms in processed foods. Sony, Matsushita, and Philips, the first three companies to commercialize videocassette recorders, were all very large; see Richard S. Rosenbloom and William J. Abernathy, "The Climate for Innovation in Industry," *Research Policy II,* August 1982, pp. 215, 217. In semiconductors, IBM, GE, RCA, and Philco were large firms, and Texas Instruments and Fairchild were small ones; see John E. Tilton, *International Diffusion of Technology: The Case of Semiconductors* (Washington, DC: Brookings Institution, 1971). For the food study, see Robert D. Buzzell and Robert E. Nourse, *Product Innovation in Food Processing: 1954–1964* (Boston: Harvard Business School Division of Research, 1967).

26. M. E. Porter, "The Technological Dimension of Competitive Strategy," in R. S. Rosenbloom, ed., *Research on Technological Innovation, Management and Policy,* vol. 1 (Greenwich, CT: JAI Press, 1983), pp. 1–33.

CHAPTER 5

1. This chapter is a revision of Robert B. Stobaugh and Phillip L. Townsend, "Price Forecasting and Strategic Planning: The Case of Petrochemicals," *Journal of Marketing Research,* February 1975, which contains the statistical test of the model. The analysis holds constant the effects of the other variables.

2. For the Du Pont study, see S. A. Billon and W. D. Robinson, "Price-Cost Relationships: Industrial Chemicals," *Proceedings,* Fall Conference, American Marketing Association, 1970. For a discussion of the decay of profit margins, see D. M. Tacke and H. C. Thorne, "Predict Prices with Inflation," *Hydrocarbon Processing,* April 1976, p. 156.

Marvin B. Lieberman, "The Learning Curve and Pricing in the Chemical Process Industries," *Rand Journal of Economics,* Summer 1984, pp. 213–228, found a sharp contrast in price behavior over short periods of time (three years) between low- and high-concentration markets; low-concentration markets were more susceptible to price declines caused by the addition of new plants. But he found no difference in price behavior over longer periods of time (8 to 21 years). For his measure of market concentration, Lieberman used the Herfindahl index, a statistical measure of the number of equal-sized competitors in a market. Lieberman found a break point at five or fewer equal-sized competitors, which means that there were likely to have been slightly more than five, since it is unlikely that all competitors would have been equal in size. To illustrate, the Herfindahl index would indicate five equal-sized competitors for a market in which six firms had the following market shares: 8 percent, 8 percent, 26 percent, 20 percent, 20 percent, and 20 percent.

A recent study found that prices are more rigid (in both upward and downward movements) in highly concentrated markets than in others; see Dennis W. Carlton, "The Rigidity of Price," *American Economic Review*, September 1986, pp. 637–658.

3. I had done extensive economic and engineering studies of styrene monomer manufacture as an employee of Monsanto Company between 1959 and 1965. Of course, the study reported here was based on published data, not Monsanto's. Also, see R. Stobaugh, *Petrochemical Manufacturing and Marketing Guide*, vol. 1 (Houston: Gulf Publishing, 1966), chap. 3.

4. Lieberman found that the entry of new competitors was significant in explaining price declines in high-concentration markets. This effect was short term (three-year period); Lieberman, "The Learning Curve and Pricing in the Chemical Process Industries," pp. 222–223. See also Richard E. Caves, "Industrial Organization, Corporate Strategy and Structure," *Journal of Economic Literature*, March 1980, pp. 77, 89.

5. The statistical test of the 82 petrochemicals includes decreases as well as increases in the number of competitors. Managers certainly believe that the departure of firms causes prices to be higher than they would otherwise be; for example, price increases in Europe in 1984 were attributed to the smaller number of competitors than had existed in the early 1980s.

6. Lieberman, for example, found that in the short run (three-year periods), a low level of capacity utilization resulted in lower prices, especially in low-concentration markets for products with a high level of capital intensity in the production facilities. Lieberman, "The Learning Curve and Pricing in the Chemical Process Industries," pp. 223–224.

7. See notes 3 and 6, chapter 1, above.

8. Thus, the measure of standardization in the statistical analysis is cross-sectional among products rather than chronological for each product.

9. It is my impression that a greater portion of the output of older plastics—polystyrene, for example—is of standardized quality than that of the newer plastics—acrylonitrile-butadiene-styrene, for example. I know of no systematic study of the subject, but interviews with industry executives and consultants confirm this conclusion.

10. T. P. Wright, "Factors Affecting the Cost of Airplanes," *Journal of Aeronautical Sciences*, February 1936, pp. 122–128; W. B. Hirschmann, "Profit from the Learning Curve," *Harvard Business Review*, January–February 1964, p. 129. For an example of cumulative production as the only explanatory variable, see Boston Consulting Group, "Perspectives on Experience," Technical Report, Boston, 1972. Lieberman, "The Learning Curve and Pricing in the Chemical Process Industries," p. 216, follows the definition adopted here and uses a separate measure for plant scale. To differentiate between the two factors, economists sometimes refer to learning as "dynamic scale economies" and to cost reductions due to larger plants as "static scale economies"; see G. Hufbauer, *Synthetic Materials and the Theory of International Trade* (Cambridge, MA: Harvard University Press, 1966), pp. 46–49. See also J. M. Dutton, A. Thomas, and J. E. Butler, "The History of Progress Functions as a Managerial Technology," *Business History Review*, Summer 1984, pp. 204–233. For detailed studies of process improvements, see Samuel Hollander, *The Sources of Increased Efficiency: A Study of Du Pont Rayon Plants* (Cambridge, MA: MIT Press, 1965), and J. Enos, *Petroleum*

Progress and Profits: A History of Process Innovation (Cambridge, MA: MIT Press, 1962).

11. Lieberman, "The Learning Curve and Pricing in the Chemical Process Industries," pp. 226–227.

12. Ibid., pp. 222–223. As mentioned in note 2, above, Lieberman found the break point between highly competitive and not-so-competitive markets to be five or fewer equal-sized competitors.

13. Phillip Townsend, *The Impact of Energy Costs, Environmentalism, and Technological Change upon the Competition between 7 Commodity Thermoplastics and Paper, Glass, Aluminum, Steel, Wood, and Textiles* (Enfield, CT, and Lexington, MA: DeBell & Richardson, and Phillip Townsend Associates, 1974); Phillip Townsend, *The Impact of Energy Costs, Technological Change & Capital Equipment Costs upon Raw Materials Competition 1978–1983–1988* (Houston: Phillip Townsend Associates, 1979); and Phillip Townsend, *The Impact of Energy Costs, Technological Change & Capital Equipment Costs upon Raw Materials Competition 1980–1985–1990* (Houston: Phillip Townsend Associates, 1980), an update of the 1978 edition. For another study that found that the experience curve applied to several products that are among the 82, see D. M. Nathanson, "The Use and Limitations of Experience Curves in Forecasting Petrochemical Prices," *Proceedings,* Annual Meeting, American Institute of Chemical Engineers, February 1972.

14. Edwin Mansfield, "How Rapidly Does New Industrial Technology Leak Out?" *Journal of Industrial Economics,* December 1985, pp. 217–223. If information acquired through learning diffuses rapidly across multiple plants belonging to the same firm, but only slowly (if at all) across plants belonging to different firms, then for a given number of industry plants, cost reduction should be more rapid if production is controlled by a smaller number of firms. The fact that Lieberman found no evidence of this effect suggests a high rate of information diffusion across firms; Lieberman, "The Learning Curve and Pricing in the Chemical Process Industries," p. 226.

15. Hufbauer, *Synthetic Materials and the Theory of International Trade.* The formula to calculate the capital cost per unit of product in a large plant vs. a small plant is: Capital Cost Plant 2 = (Size Plant 2 ÷ Size Plant 1)$^{0.6}$ × Capital Cost Plant 1, although the 0.6 factor varies somewhat (usually between 0.5 to 0.7) for petrochemicals. See also, John Haldi and David Whitcomb, "Economics of Scale in Industrial Plants," *Journal of Political Economy,* August 1967, pp. 375–385. For a discussion of transport costs and other constraints on plant size, see F. M. Scherer et al., *The Economics of Multi-Plant Operation: An International Comparisons Study* (Cambridge, MA: Harvard University Press, 1975).

16. One study indicates that growth in new plant size appears to have been driven by steady technological progress over time rather than by market concentration, market growth, or the magnitude of investment scale economies; see Marvin B. Lieberman, "Market Growth, Economies of Scale, and Capacity Expansion in the Chemical Processing Industries," *Journal of Industrial Economics* (forthcoming). These findings are consistent with the idea that technological progress can lead to shifts in the scale frontier; for evidence on this point in the steel industry, see Pedro Nueno, "A Comparative Study of the Capacity Decision Process in the Steel Industry: The U.S. and Europe" (DBA thesis, Harvard Business School, 1973), chap. III. For the methanol example, see Barry Hedley, Walter Powers, and Robert Stobaugh, "Methanol: How, Where, Who—Future," *Hydrocarbon Processing,* September 1970, p. 276.

17. Capacity data and operating rates for individual plants making the individual petro-

chemicals are either unavailable or extremely difficult to collect. A usable substitution is average production per manufacturer. Typically, a manufacturer has no more than several plants in the United States, and often just one, to produce a given petrochemical. Furthermore, most petrochemical plants operate at relatively high rates of capacity.

The use of this proxy variable is consistent with the observation that other economies of scale apply to the company capacity as opposed to plant capacity. For a given company, selling, technical support, and administrative overheads increase less rapidly than production; thus, the use of average production per manufacturer as a proxy variable, in addition to measuring average plant size, also takes into account lower overhead costs that occur when a company increases its output of a given product, regardless of whether its average plant size is changing. There is a potential complication in the analysis if one uses average output per producer rather than output of the largest producer. In the case of severe price competition (when some producers are operating at a loss), one might expect the pricing to be more heavily impacted by the size of the largest (and hence lowest-cost) plant than by the average-scale economies of all producers. Nevertheless, both variables have tended to increase at the same time and average production per producer is the best estimate of scale that is readily available for a large number of petrochemicals.

18. Pricing strategy, of course, should be coordinated with the capacity strategy. There is an extensive literature on this subject; for example, see J. T. Wenders, "Excess Capacity as a Barrier to Entry," *Journal of Industrial Economics,* November 1971, pp. 14–19; A. M. Spence, "Entry Capacity, Investment and Oligopolistic Pricing," *Bell Journal of Economics,* Autumn 1977, pp. 534–544; A. M. Spence, "The Learning Curve and Competition," *Bell Journal of Economics,* Spring 1981, pp. 49–70; M. Lieberman, "Excess Capacity as a Barrier to Entry: An Empirical Appraisal," *Journal of Industrial Economics,* June 1987, pp. 607–627; R. J. Gilbert and M. Lieberman, "Investment and Coordination in Oligopolistic Industries," *Rand Journal of Economics,* Spring 1987, pp. 17–33; and M. Lieberman, "Investment Strategies for Capacity Expansion," *Sloan Management Review,* Summer 1987. For other discussions of optimal pricing in a dynamic situation, see J. S. Bain, "A Note on Pricing in Monopoly and Oligopoly," *American Economic Review,* March 1949, pp. 448–464; J. S. Bain, *Barriers to New Competition* (Cambridge, MA: Harvard University Press, 1956); M. Porter, *Competitive Strategy* (New York: Free Press, 1980); D. J. Teece, "Economic Analysis and Strategic Management," *California Management Review,* Spring 1984, pp. 87–110; P. Ghemawat, "Building Strategy on the Experience Curve," *Harvard Business Review,* March–April 1985, pp. 143–149; and M. Lieberman, "The Learning Curve, Diffusion, and Competitive Strategy," *Strategic Management Journal* (forthcoming).

CHAPTER 6

1. *Forbes,* July 15, 1985, p. 91.

2. *Business Week,* May 23, 1977, p. 106B.

3. The conclusions are supported by interviews, by the sizes of the coefficients in a multiple regression model available from the author, and by the data in Figure 6-3. The multiple regression model holds constant the effects of the other variables.

4. A theoretical treatment of the decision to license or not license indicates that if two firms are Cournot duopolists, if the owner of the technology can implement a two-part tariff licensing contract in which the licensee pays both a fixed fee and a per-unit charge for product manufactured, and if the licensee produces positive output in the absence of the license, then the technology owner would always license. The authors conclude, however, that under some assumed competitive conditions, the contract would induce such collusive behavior by the two firms that it would be held illegal by antitrust authorities. See Michael L. Katz and Carl Shapiro, "On the Licensing of Innovations," *Rand Journal of Economics,* Winter 1985, pp. 504–520 (esp. pp. 511–513). For a discussion of coalitions, including joint ventures and licensing, see Michael E. Porter and Mark B. Fuller, "Coalitions and Global Strategy," and Pankaj Ghemawat, Michael E. Porter, and Richard A. Rawlinson, "Patterns of International Coalition Activity," in Michael E. Porter, ed., *Competition in Global Industries* (Boston: Harvard Business School Press, 1986), pp. 315–343, 345–365.

5. For example, Beta, in chapter 3, above, faced this situation.

6. The basic argument is that under certain conditions (such as nonincreasing returns to scale), the coordination of interdependent activities by a complete set of perfectly competitive markets (which by definition contains a large number of buyers and sellers, perfect information, and so on) cannot be improved upon; in such cases, there would be no advantage in replacing a perfect system of markets by a centrally administered control system. For a fuller discussion, see P. J. Buckley and M. Casson, *The Future of the Multinational Enterprise* (New York: Holmes and Meier, 1976), chap. 2. Note that Buckley and Casson treat loss due to a price reduction because of additional competition as a special case of uncertainty. For related theories see O. E. Williamson, "The Modern Corporation: Origins, Evolution, Attributes," *Journal of Economic Literature,* December 1981, pp. 1537–1568, for a view of the corporation's vertical integration decision that emphasizes economizing on transaction costs; and A. M. Rugman, ed., *New Theories of the Multinational Enterprise* (New York: St. Martin's Press, 1982), for a discussion of the theory of internationalization that seeks to explain three modes of international operations—trade, foreign direct investment, and licensing— by multinational enterprises. For a succinct review of the literature on licensing versus investment, see R. E. Caves, *Multinational Enterprise and Economic Analysis* (Cambridge: Cambridge University Press, 1982), pp. 204–207. Also, see S. Magee, "Information and the MNC: An Appropriability Theory of Direct Foreign Investment," in J. N. Bhagwati, ed., *The New International Economic Order* (Cambridge, MA: MIT Press, 1977), pp. 317–340; D. J. Teece, "Technological and Organization Factors in the Theory of the Multinational Enterprise," in M. Casson, ed., *The Growth of International Business* (London: George Allen & Unwin, 1983), pp. 51–62; Nancy T. Gallini and Ralph A. Winter, "Licensing in the Theory of Innovation," *Rand Journal of Economics,* Summer 1985, pp. 237–252; W. H. Davidson and D. G. McFetridge, "Key Characteristics in the Choice of International Technology Transfer Mode," *Journal of International Business Studies,* Summer 1985, pp. 5–21; F. J. Contractor, "A Generalized Theorem for Joint-Venture and Licensing Negotiations," *Journal of International Business Studies,* Summer 1985, pp. 23–50, and *Licensing in International Strategy: A Guide for Planning and Negotiations* (Westport, CT: Quorum Books, 1985); K. J. Hladik, *International Joint Ventures: An Economic Analysis of U.S.-Foreign Business Partnerships* (Lexington, MA: Lexington Books, 1985); and E. Anderson and H. Gatignon, "Modes of Foreign Entry: A Transaction Cost Analysis and Propositions," *Journal of International Business Studies,* Fall 1986, pp. 1–26.
    The pattern of petrochemicals described in this chapter is consistent with findings from a variety of U.S. industries that licensing and joint ventures become more important channels relative to wholly owned subsidiaries as the technology gets older. See E. Mansfield, A. Romeo, and S. Wagner, "Foreign Trade and U.S. Research and Development," *Review of Economics and Statistics,* February 1979, pp. 49–57; and E. Mans-

field and A. Romeo, "Technology Transfer to Overseas Subsidiaries by U.S.-based Firms," *Quarterly Journal of Economics,* December 1980, pp. 737–750. For evidence that bargaining decisions change with number of participants, see Lawrence Fouraker and Sidney Siegel, *Bargaining Behavior* (New York: McGraw-Hill, 1963), pp. 165, 199, 209–210.

7. For evidence that when there is no standard method available for dividing a sum, the participants perceive that a 50-50 split is fair, see Lawrence Fouraker and Sidney Siegel, *Bargaining and Group Decision-Making* (New York: McGraw-Hill, 1960), pp. 74–76, 85–90.

8. For Du Pont example, see David A. Hounshell and John K. Smith, *Science and Corporate Strategy: R&D at Du Pont, 1902–1980* (Cambridge: Cambridge University Press, 1987), chap. 19. Other examples are taken from interviews with industry executives and consultants.

9. A statistical analysis is available from the author of this book; see note 3, above.

10. In statistical terms, the probability that small firms are more likely to transfer technology through a sale rather than internal use is greater than .999 for either international or domestic transfers, with the effects of the other variables held constant, but the size of the standardized coefficient for firm size in the equation with *international* transfers of technology is twice as large as in the equation that includes *domestic* as well as international transfers. A statistical analysis is available from the author; see note 3, above.

11. The domestic/international transfer is also included in the statistical model; see note 3, above. A comparison of motivations to license domestically versus overseas is in Pankaj Ghemewat, "Capacity Expansion in the Titanium Dioxide Industry," *Journal of Industrial Economics,* December 1984, pp. 145–163. For examples of misjudgment of factors involved in foreign direct investments, see R. B. Stobaugh et al., *Nine Investments Abroad and Their Impact at Home* (Boston: Harvard Business School Division of Research, 1976).

12. J. M. Stopford and L. T. Wells, Jr., *Managing the Multinational Enterprise* (New York: Basic Books, 1972), p. 150.

13. R. Vernon, *Storm over the Multinationals* (Cambridge, MA: Harvard University Press, 1977).

14. A statistical analysis is available from the author of this book; see note 3, above.

15. Piero Telesio, "Foreign Licensing in Multinational Enterprises," in R. Stobaugh and L. Wells, Jr., eds., *Technology Crossing Borders,* (Boston: Harvard Business School Press, 1984), pp. 177–201, also found this in his interviews. Also see Davidson and McFetridge, "Key Characteristics in the Choice of International Technology Transfer Mode."

16. Although I did not search explicitly for the reciprocity licensing reported by Telesio (see note 15), I noticed for all nine products only one sale of technology that was the result of a reciprocity agreement—Du Pont's sale of cyclohexane technology to Imperial Chemical Industries in 1949.

17. These conclusions were not derived from one overall regression model, as were the conclusions for the licensing versus investment decision, but from several different sources: Figure 6-3 in this chapter, and R. B. Stobaugh, "The Product Life Cycle, U.S.

Exports, and International Investment," DBA dissertation, Harvard Business School, 1968, pp. 149–150. See also Stopford and Wells, *Managing the Multinational Enterprise,* part II.

CHAPTER 7

1. John E. Tilton, *International Diffusion of Technology: The Case of Semiconductors* (Washington, DC: Brookings Institution, 1971).

2. G. C. Hufbauer used the term "pecking order" in his *Synthetic Materials and the Theory of International Trade* (Cambridge, MA: Harvard University Press, 1966). The seminal article in a large body of literature dealing with products in general—not just petrochemicals—is R. Vernon, "International Investment and International Trade in the Product Cycle," *Quarterly Journal of Economics,* May 1966, pp. 190–207. For other studies of determinants of locations of foreign manufacturing facilities for products in general, see L. Otterbeck, *Location and Strategic Planning: Towards a Contingency Theory of Industrial Location* (Stockholm: Economic Research Institute, Stockholm School of Economics, 1973); F. Knickerbocker, *Oligopolistic Reaction and Multinational Enterprise* (Boston: Harvard Business School Division of Research, 1973); E. Graham, "Oligopolistic Imitation and European Direct Investment in the United States," DBA thesis, Harvard Business School, 1974; R. Vernon, "The Location of Economic Activity," in J. H. Dunning, ed., *Economic Analysis and Multinational Enterprise* (London: George Allen & Unwin, 1974); Hans Schollhammer, "Locational Strategies of Multinational Firms," Study No. 1, Pepperdine University Center for International Business, Los Angeles, 1974; F. Scherer et al., *The Economics of Multi-Plant Operation* (Cambridge, MA: Harvard University Press, 1975); S. Hirsch, "An International Trade and Investment Theory of the Firm," *Oxford Economic Papers,* July 1976, pp. 258–270; W. Isard, "Location Theory, Agglomeration and the Pattern of World Trade," in B. G. Ohlin, ed., *The International Allocation of Economic Activity* (New York: Holmes and Meier, 1977); R. Vernon, *Storm over the Multinationals* (Cambridge, MA: Harvard University Press, 1977); S. P. Magee, "Multinational Corporations: The Industry Technology Cycle and Development," *Journal of World Trade Law,* July–August 1977, pp. 297–321; J. H. Dunning, "Explaining Changing Patterns of International Production: In Defense of the Eclectic Theory," *Oxford Bulletin of Economics and Statistics,* November 1979, pp. 269–295; R. Grosse, *Foreign Investment Codes and Location of Direct Investment* (New York: Praeger, 1980), chap. 3; R. Grosse, *The Theory of Foreign Direct Investment* (Colombia, SC: Essays in International Business, College of Business Administration, University of South Carolina, 1981); and I. B. Kravis and R. E. Lipsey, "The Location of Overseas Production and Production for Export by U.S. Multinational Firms," *Journal of International Economics,* May 1982, pp. 201–223.

3. See John G. McLean, "Financing Overseas Expansion," *Harvard Business Review,* March–April 1963, p. 53.

4. A statistical analysis is available from the author of this book. The analysis holds constant the effects of the other variables.

5. Interviews with executives in the 1960s and 1970s.

6. See note 4, above.

7. F. R. Root, "U.S. Business Abroad and Political Risks," *MSU Business Topics,* Winter

1968, pp. 73–80; S. F. Robock, "Political Risk: Identification and Assessment," *Columbia Journal of World Business,* January–February 1972, pp. 6–20; S. J. Kobrin, "Environmental Determinants of F.D.I.," *Journal of International Business,* Fall–Winter 1976, pp. 29–42; L. H. Thunnell, *Political Risks in International Business: Investment Behavior of Multinational Corporations* (New York: Praeger, 1977); R. J. Rummel and D. A. Heenan, "How Multinationals Analyze Political Risk," *Harvard Business Review,* January–February 1978, pp. 67–76; S. J. Kobrin, "Political Risk: A Review and Reconsideration," *Journal of International Business,* Spring–Summer 1979, pp. 67–80; S. J. Kobrin, "Political Assessment by International Firms: Models or Methodologies?" *Journal of Policy Modeling,* May 1981, pp. 251–270; T. H. Moran, "Overview: International Political Risk Assessment," in *International Political Risk Assessment: The State of the Art,* T. H. Moran, ed., Landegger Papers in International Business and Public Policy, School of Foreign Service, Georgetown University, Washington, DC, n.d. [ca. 1981]; J. D. Simon, "Political Risk Assessment: Past Trends and Future Prospects," *Columbia Journal of World Business,* Fall 1982, pp. 62–71; F. Ghadar, S. J. Kobrin, and T. H. Moran, eds., *Managing International Political Risk: Strategies and Techniques* (Washington, DC: Landegger Program in International Business Diplomacy, Georgetown University, 1983).

8. For an early work that gave an example of how corporate decision makers could focus on key variables affecting individual projects, see R. Stobaugh, "How to Analyze Foreign Investment Climates," *Harvard Business Review,* September–October 1969, pp. 100–108. For a recent article that focuses on company-specific risks, see J. E. Austin and D. B. Yoffie, "Political Forecasting as a Management Tool," *Journal of Forecasting,* October–December 1984, pp. 395–408.

9. See note 4, above.

10. See note 4, above.

11. Nations typically do not publish export and import data on individual petrochemicals until they have been manufactured for many years, so data for the early years come from consulting firms. Trade data were available only for the United States.

12. Export data were not available for isoprene.

13. Trade data for the U.S. petrochemical industry were not available for years prior to the early 1970s and hence were not available for the years in which the export peaks were reached for these products. Still, the export peaks of these products were higher than those subsequently registered by the petrochemical industry; U.S. exports of petrochemicals ranged from 10 to 16 percent of U.S. petrochemical shipments between 1973 and 1985; see Figure 9-3. The U.S. chemical industry exported $2.4 billion out of total sales of $36 billion in 1965, or 6.7 percent according to *The Chemical Industry* (Paris: OECD, 1967), pp. 16, 143. The ratio of U.S. chemical exports to total U.S. chemical industry sales for the years 1929, 1939, 1948, 1957, and 1961 varied from 4 percent to 6 percent; Jules Backman, *Foreign Competition in Chemicals and Allied Products* (Washington, DC: Manufacturing Chemists Association, 1965), p. 6. U.S. exports as a percentage of U.S. production would be less than these percentages because these are a percentage of industry sales, which are lower than total production because of captive uses of some of the output by manufacturers.

14. Jacob Viner, "Cost Curves and Supply Curves," *Zeitschrift für Nationalökonomie,* September 1931, pp. 23–46; reprinted with supplementary note, in American Economic Association, *Readings in Price Theory* (Homewood, IL: Richard D. Irwin, 1952), pp. 198–233; George Stigler, "Production and Distribution in the Short Run," *Journal of Political Economy,* June 1939, pp. 305–327; Alan S. Manne, ed., *Invest-*

ments for Capacity Expansion: Size, Location and Time Phasing (London: George Allen & Unwin, 1967), pp. 44–45; and John Haldi and David Whitcomb, "Economies of Scale in Industrial Plants," *Journal of Political Economy,* August 1967, pp. 373–385.

15. A 440-million-pound-per-year styrene plant by BASF, *Oil Paint & Drug Reporter* (now *Chemical Marketing Reporter*), April 18, 1966, p. 9.

16. James Brander and Paul Krugman, "A 'Reciprocal Dumping' Model of International Trade," *Journal of International Economics,* November 1983, pp. 313–321.

17. For quantities of exports and imports of a number of countries, see "Chem-Intell Trade and Production Statistics Data Base" (London: Chemical Intelligence Services, a Division of Reed Telepublishing Ltd.). For a comparison of U.S. export and U.S. domestic prices, see Bureau of Census, *United States Exports of Domestic and Foreign Merchandise.* For U.S. domestic prices, see United States International Trade Commission, *Synthetic Organic Chemicals United States Production and Sales.* Information on behavior of oligopolists is from interviews with executives. Multipoint competitors are not necessarily more able to moderate their rivalry than are singlepoint competitors; the outcome depends on specific parameters, see Jeremy I. Bulow, John D. Geanakoplos, and Paul D. Klemperer, "Multimarket Oligopoly: Strategic Substitutes and Complements," *Journal of Political Economy,* June 1985, pp. 488–511.

18. Interviews with executives.

19. *Oil, Paint & Drug Reporter* (now *Chemical Marketing Reporter*), February 9, 1959, p. 45.

20. House Committee on Ways and Means, *Foreign Trade and Tariff Proposals,* Hearings, 90th Cong., July 1, 1968, pp. 4536 and 4559.

21. *Chemical Week,* March 14, 1973, p. 24, and *Chemical Marketing Reporter,* March 19, 1973, p. 3. One study suggests that balancing exports, as defined by me, account for perhaps one-third of world trade in petrochemicals, see George B. Hegeman, "World Chemical Trade—Expectations and Realities," a paper presented to the American Chemical Society, New York, August 24, 1981, mimeograph, available from G. Hegeman, Arthur D. Little, Inc., Cambridge, MA. Hegeman uses five trade classifications instead of my two.

CHAPTER 8

1. Raymond E. Kirk and Donald F. Othmer, *Encyclopedia of Chemical Technology* (New York: Wiley, 1963) 2d ed., vol. 13, p. 370.

2. One source claims that methanol was produced commercially as early as the 1600s, but does not cite a reference for that statement. See American Chemical Society, "Chemistry in the Economy," Washington, DC, 1973, p. 31.

3. Ibid.

4. Kirk and Othmer, *Encyclopedia of Chemical Technology,* vol. 9, p. 39, put the start-up date for both plants at 1927, but private correspondence with Du Pont and the following source indicates that Du Pont was the first U.S. producer of synthetic methanol, in

1926, with Commercial Solvents following in 1927; see William Haynes, *American Chemical Industry,* vol. 4 (New York: Van Nostrand, 1948), pp. 176–177.

5. *Oil and Gas Journal,* February 12, 1968, p. 106.

6. Barry Hedley, Walter Powers, and Robert B. Stobaugh, "Methanol: How, Where, Who—Future," *Hydrocarbon Processing,* September 1970, p. 277. One trade journal article introduced ICI's process by saying, "Forget everything you know about making methanol. This new process changes it all": *Chemical Week,* January 6, 1968, p. 34. Another journal said, "Some Europeans working with methanol processes apparently have not gotten word that they are supposed to be suffering from a technology gap": *Oil and Gas Journal,* February 26, 1968, p. 51.

7. Taesung was actually the first company to buy the technology, in 1968, but the company's 150-ton-per-day plant did not come onstream until 1971. *Chemical Week,* May 11, 1968, p. 28.

8. As of 1984, ICI's low-pressure technology was being used in 16 countries, all of whom had one plant using ICI technology, except for the United States (5), Canada (4), the Netherlands (2), and the Soviet Union (2). The figure would have been higher had a number of plants in Western Europe and Japan, built in the early 1970s, not closed. Chemical Intelligence Service files, plus review of trade journals, especially *Chemical Marketing Reporter, European Chemical News,* and *Hydrocarbon Processing.*

9. Of the free-world plants that were operating in 1967, ICI had supplied technology to seven, including its own three plants. Montecatini (later Montedison, via a merger with Edison), which had developed its own technology and become Italy's first synthetic methanol producer in 1934, had also supplied technology for seven plants operating in 1967, including one fully owned and one partially owned plant in Italy. Other leading methanol technology licensors, none of whom were producers, were Chemico (U.S.), Ammonia Casale (Italy), Vulcan (U.S.), and Inventa (Switzerland).

10. *Chemical Week,* April 22, 1967, p. 134.

11. *Chemical Week,* May 7, 1966, p. 56.

12. *Chemical Week,* July 1, 1961, p. 56.

13. *Oil, Paint & Drug Reporter* (now *Chemical Marketing Reporter*), January 17, 1966, p. 31.

CHAPTER 9

1. Although the experiences of the nine products both before and after 1973 mirrored that of the industry, some of the changes were larger for the nine products. This fact is not surprising, because all nine products are primary and intermediate petrochemicals; hence, they are more affected than the petrochemical industry as a whole by changes in raw material prices. The industry includes plastics, fibers, and elastomers, which are farther down the processing chain, where product prices are less sensitive to changes in raw material costs. Still, the changes in the nine products in the twelve-year period before and after 1973 were identical in direction to those of the petrochemical industry.

Unless otherwise noted, all U.S. data on production, price, and number of manufac-
turers for the nine products are from U.S. International Trade Commission, *Synthetic
Organic Chemicals—U.S. Production and Sales* (Washington, DC: GPO) annual, with
import and export data from U.S. Department of Commerce, Bureau of the Census,
U.S. Imports for Consumption and General Imports, FT246/Annual (Washington,
DC: GPO), various years, and U.S. Department of Commerce, Bureau of the Census,
U.S. Exports Schedule B Commodity by Country, FT446/Annual (Washington, DC:
GPO), various years. Any inflation correction was done using the GNP deflator.

2. Corrected for inflation, the average was 68 percent.
   Price indices are not available for the petrochemical industry prior to 1972, but a
   review of price indices for categories of chemical and allied products that consist
   largely of petrochemicals, such as industrial organic chemicals, reveals a price decline
   in both real and nominal terms. See U.S. Department of Commerce, *U.S. Industrial
   Outlook* (Washington, DC: GPO), various years.

3. The increase in consumption is given in constant dollars. Although in some cases, data
   are for "all petrochemical products" and in other cases for "the petrochemical industry," the differences for the purposes of this book are negligible. See U.S. Department
   of Commerce, *U.S. Industrial Outlook,* various years.
   The average growth in consumption of the nine products during this period in the
   United States was 14 percent yearly, or somewhat above the rate for the industry as a
   whole—not surprising, since some of the nine products were in an early stage of their
   life cycles when market growth is very rapid.
   In Western Europe, the total annual growth rate for petrochemicals during this
   period was about double that in the United States, while the growth rate in Japan was
   even higher than in Western Europe; see Ir. E. Lelyveld (Shell Internationale Chemie
   Maatschappij N.V.), "The State of the West European Petrochemical Industry," a
   paper given to the European Petrochemical Association meeting at Monte Carlo, October 16, 1972.

4. For the nine products, the average price increase was 145 percent.

5. For the nine products, 20 percent.

6. Phillip Townsend, *The Impact of Energy Costs, Environmentalism, and Technological
   Change upon the Competition between 7 Commodity Thermoplastics and Paper,
   Glass, Aluminum, Steel, Wood, and Textiles* (Enfield, CT, and Lexington, MA: DeBell
   & Richardson and Phillip Townsend Associates, 1974).

7. For the nine products, 66 percent.

8. Industry executive quoted in *Chemical Marketing Reporter,* August 16, 1976, p. 14.
   Methanol operating rate from data from Chem Systems, 1985.

9. For the nine products, 85 percent.

10. "Investment Forecasts for Chemical Commodities," *Chemical Engineering Progress,*
    August 1981, pp. 11–18.

11. For the nine products, 27 percent.

12. Operating rates come from Federal Reserve Board, and from Standard & Poor's *Indus-
    try Surveys, Chemicals,* October 24, 1985, p. 17; profit data from Compustat financial
    data base, as reported in U.S. Department of Commerce, *A Competitive Assessment of
    the U.S. Petrochemical Industry* (Washington, DC: August 31, 1982), section II, pp.

21, 27; and *Petroleum Economist,* July 1985, p. 239. For estimates of losses, see *Chemical Marketing Reporter,* October 18, 1982, p. 3; and *The Economist,* November 6, 1982, p. 18 and November 13, 1982, p. 61.

The profit picture for manufacturers of the nine products was also bleak during the early 1980s. The average margin of the price of the nine products over the cost of petroleum feedstock was about the same in 1982 as it had been in 1978, just prior to the increase in crude oil prices. Roaring inflation, however, had the effect of reducing the margin in real terms by 28 percent.

13. *Forbes,* February 28, 1983, pp. 98–99.

14. Interviews with industry executives and consulting firms.

15. For eight of the nine products for which data were available from a consulting firm (data for isoprene were not available), the average capacity of the U.S. plants per product that were shut down between 1979 and 1983 (and were not operating in 1983) was 55 percent of the capacity of those remaining in operation between 1979 and 1983. In most cases, one company owned only one facility in the United States, so that the shutdown of smaller facilities meant the exiting of the industry by the smaller competitors.

    Twenty-nine plants were shut down while 68 plants continued to operate; six new plants were added, with capacities averaging 115 percent of the plants that operated throughout the 1979–1983 period. Thus, overall U.S. capacity dropped only about 10 percent. Data from Phillip Townsend Associates, Houston, TX.

    For a theoretical analysis of the circumstances under which firms with different capacities are likely to be able to "hang on" longer profitably when the market is declining, see Pankaj Ghemawat and Barry Nalebuff, "Exit," *Rand Journal of Economics,* Summer 1985, pp. 184–194.

16. Joseph L. Bower, *When Markets Quake: The Management Challenge of Restructuring Industry* (Boston: Harvard Business School Press, 1986), pp. 130–135 (BP/ICI swap) and p. 75 (quote); also see Organization for Economic Co-operation and Development [OECD], *Petrochemical Industry: Energy Aspects of Structural Change* (Paris: 1985).

17. For a concise summary of Dow's "restructuring" see *Chemical Insight,* Late March 1986, pp. 3–4. For an interview with Oreffice, including the statement quoted here, see James Gagne, "The U.S. CPI Will Change Dramatically but Remain No. 1 in the World," *CPI Purchasing,* March 1985, pp. 33–35.

18. For the nine products, 19 percent.

19. Phillip Townsend, *The Impact of Energy Costs, Environmentalism, and Technological Change upon the Competition between 7 Commodity Thermoplastics and Paper, Glass, Aluminum, Steel, Wood, and Textiles* (Enfield, CT, and Lexington, MA: DeBell & Richardson and Phillip Townsend Associates, 1974); Phillip Townsend, *The Impact of Energy Costs, Technological Change & Capital Equipment Costs upon Raw Materials Competition 1978–1983–1988* (Houston: Phillip Townsend Associates, 1979); and Phillip Townsend, *The Impact of Energy Costs, Technological Change & Capital Equipment Costs upon Raw Materials Competition 1980–1985–1990,* an update of the 1979 ed. (Houston: Phillip Townsend Associates, 1980).

20. Michael E. Porter, "The Technological Dimension of Competitive Strategy," in Richard S. Rosenbloom, *Research on Technological Innovation, Management and Policy,* vol. 1 (Greenwich, CT: JAI Press, 1983), pp. 1–33.

21. The first study was reported by Charles Doscher, ENI Chemical president; see *World*

Petrochemical Analysis, December 13, 1984, p. 18. The second study, by C. H. Kline & Co., was reported in their *Chemical Strategies* in late 1982.

22. My classifications, using criteria in my chapter 2 after a review of trade literature, including *Hydrocarbon Processing* annual "Petrochemical Handbook" issues; special reports, such as SRI International, *Chemical Economics Handbook,* "CEH Marketing Report, Methanol," October 1983, pp. 674.5022, L–N; and R. E. Kirk and D. F. Othmer, *Encyclopedia of Chemical Technology* (New York: Interscience Encyclopedia, various issues).

23. *Chemical Economics Handbook,* pp. 674.5022, L–N.

24. Chemical Intelligence Services files plus review of trade journals, especially *Chemical Marketing Reporter, European Chemical News,* and *Hydrocarbon Processing,* and Kirk and Othmer, *Encyclopedia of Chemical Technology.* These numbers are for the world other than the Centrally Planned Economies (CPEs); incomplete data for the CPEs indicate that more than 90 percent of their technology for manufacturing the nine products during this period was purchased.

25. "Worldwide Listing of Process Technology Available for License," *European Chemical News ECN Process Supplement,* November 1985, pp. 27–41; and "Petrochemical Handbook" issues of *Hydrocarbon Processing,* various years. Union Carbide licensed its new and highly efficient linear low-density polyethylene Unipol process to a number of firms, including Al-Jubail Petrochemical Company in Saudi Arabia; see Douglas Smock, "The Saudis Are Coming!" *CPI Purchasing,* March 1985, p. 49.

26. Chemical Intelligence Services files; *Chemical Marketing Reporter; European Chemical News; Hydrocarbon Processing;* Kirk and Othmer, *Encyclopedia of Chemical Technology,* plus information from Chem Systems, 1985.

27. Ibid.

28. For those readers interested in more detail on the manufacture of vinyl chloride monomer, it can be made from the cracking of ethylene dichloride, which, in turn, can be made from the reaction of chlorine and ethylene, which, in turn, can be made, respectively, from salt (using electricity, which can be generated using natural gas as a fuel) and ethane. See Kirk and Othmer, *Encyclopedia of Chemical Technology;* and David P. Keane, Robert B. Stobaugh, and Phillip L. Townsend, "Vinyl Chloride: How, Where, Who—Future," *Hydrocarbon Processing,* February 1973, pp. 99–110.

29. United States International Trade Commission, *The Probable Impact on the U.S. Petrochemical Industry of the Expanding Petrochemical Industries in the Conventional-Energy-Rich Nations,* USITC Publication 1870 (Washington, DC: GPO, April 1983), and *Potential Effects of Foreign Governments' Policies of Pricing Natural Resources,* USITC Publication 1696 (Washington, DC: GPO, May 1985).

30. For an early list of planned projects in the Middle East and North Africa, see *Chemical Marketing Reporter, Chemical Business,* January 12, 1981, pp. 36–43. For a later list of ethylene and ethylene derivative plants, existing and projected, in the Middle East and North Africa, see OECD, *Petrochemical Industry,* pp. 152–153. And for even wider geographical coverage, including Canada, see United States International Trade Commission, *The Probable Impact on the U.S. Petrochemical Industry of the Expanding Petrochemical Industries in the Conventional-Energy-Rich Nations.*

31. Information from Phillip Townsend Associates, Houston, TX.

32. The United States does not grant GSP benefits to any OPEC member unless there is a bilateral trade agreement on specific products; only Ecuador, Indonesia, and Venezuela have such an agreement. The GSP issue between the EEC and Saudi Arabia was complicated by a number of factors, including the duty-free status of certain North African countries on exports to the EEC, the duty-free status of European exports to Saudi Arabia, the possibility of Saudi retaliation against European tariffs on Saudi petrochemical exports, whether the products were to be classified by the EEC as sensitive or non-sensitive (a classification that affected the conditions under which an EEC tariff would be imposed and the speed of its imposition), the level of the EEC duty-free allowables, diplomatic relations between the EEC members and Saudi Arabia, disagreements among the member countries of the EEC and among EEC officials, negotiations between the Gulf Coordination Council (GCC) and the European Community, the possibility that preferential treatment by the EEC to the GCC would violate certain agreements with other countries, and the fact that the joint-venture owners of the Saudi facilities were American and Japanese rather than European. "Derisory" was used by Mike Hyde in his newsletter, *Chemical Insight,* Early April, 1985, p. 8. For a description of the workings of the GSP in the European Community, see *Chemical Insight,* Late March 1984, pp. 1–4. Also, see *The Economist,* July 24, 1982, p. 62, January 26, 1985, p. 68, August 3, 1985, p. 62, and January 18, 1986, p. 59; *World Petrochemical Analysis,* August 9, 1984, pp. 1–3, December 13, 1984, pp. 17–18, February 7, 1985, p. 1, December 13, 1985, p. 1, January 24, 1986, pp. 4–5, and April 4, 1986, pp. 1–3; *European Chemical News,* December 16, 1985, p. 11; *Chemical Marketing Reporter,* April 6, 1987, p. 36, and June 3, 1985, p. 7; *International Herald Tribune,* May 3–4, 1986, p. 3; *Petrochemical News,* September 26, 1986, p. 1; and *Chemical Insight,* Early September 1985, p. 1.

33. *Chemical Marketing Reporter,* April 6, 1986, p. 36.

34. *Chemical Marketing Reporter,* January 7, 1985, pp. 30–38.

35. U.S. Department of Commerce *U.S. Industrial Outlook, 1986* (Washington, DC: GPO, 1986), p. 11–2.
    U.S. imports of the nine products rose slightly during the years 1973–1985. From negligible levels between 1961 and 1973, they increased in 1985 to a level of 5 percent of the new supply (the sum of production plus imports, a measure used by the U.S. Department of Commerce). There was, however, a vast difference among the individual products. Resource-dependent exports from the new export-based methanol plants in hydrocarbon-rich countries, for example, caused U.S. imports of methanol to rise to 27 percent of new U.S. supply and reduced U.S. exports to negligible levels. U.S. imports of isoprene increased to 10 percent of U.S. new supply because an older, inefficient U.S. plant was closed. U.S. imports of the remaining seven products averaged only about 1.5 percent of U.S. new supply. Industry executives believed that the imports resulted from opportunistic traders taking advantage of the strong dollar. All of the products except methanol still showed a positive net trade balance (exports minus imports) in 1985.

36. For the prediction of a negative U.S. trade balance in petrochemicals (excluding specialties) by 1990, see United States International Trade Commission, *The Shift from U.S. Production of Commodity Petrochemicals to Value-Added Specialty Chemical Products and the Possible Impact on U.S. Trade,* USITC Publication 1677 (Washington, DC: GPO, April 1985). For prediction by Commerce Department official, see *Forbes,* November 7, 1983, p. 56.

CHAPTER 10

1. *Chemical Marketing Reporter,* June 13, 1977, p. 11. The potential quantity as well as the actual quantity of imports is important in affecting price.

2. Interviews with company executives.

3. For the prediction of a negative U.S. trade balance in petrochemicals (excluding specialties) by 1990, see United States International Trade Commission, *The Shift from U.S. Production of Commodity Petrochemicals to Value-Added Specialty Chemical Products and the Possible Impact on U.S. Trade,* USITC Publication 1677 (Washington, DC: GPO, April 1985). Trade data for 1986 obtained from interview with official of U.S. Department of Commerce; see also, *Chemical Week,* February 18, 1987, pp. 26–29.

4. For example, Data Resources Incorporated (DRI), a major econometric consulting firm, estimated to me in an interview in mid-1987 that the growth of petrochemical consumption in the United States would be 1.2 to 1.3 times that of U.S. GNP. U.S. production was expected to grow slightly more than this because of improvements in the U.S. trade balance resulting from the weaker dollar. For other estimates, see *Chemical Insight,* Late April 1986, pp. 1–3, and *Financial Times World Petrochemical Analysis,* April 18, 1986, pp. 1–4. For an example of the view that the petrochemical industry is mature and would grow less than GNP without the 1986 oil price drop, see Organization for Economic Cooperation and Development [OECD], *Petrochemical Industry: Energy Aspects of Structural Change* (Paris: 1985). This latter study also makes the case that the industry was approaching maturity even before the 1973 oil price shock. For the view that the OECD ɔverstated the degree of maturity, see *Chemical Insight,* Early June 1985.

5. The relationship between market growth and entry of new competitors for the 82 petrochemicals studied in chapter 5, above, is statistically significant.

6. For views that the industry will be wary about price cutting, see *Financial Times World Petrochemicals Analysis,* March 21, 1986, p. 1.

7. See chapter 7, above. An excellent summary of the product cycle hypothesis, which explains why industrialized countries have an advantage in innovating new products, appears in Raymond Vernon, "The Product Cycle Hypothesis in a New International Environment," *Oxford Bulletin,* November 1979, pp. 255–267. For more on the product cycle, see Raymond Vernon, "International Investment and International Trade in the Product Cycle," *Quarterly Journal of Economics,* May 1966, pp. 190–207; Louis T. Wells, Jr., *The Product Life Cycle and International Trade* (Boston: Harvard Business School Division of Research, 1972); and the summary in Michael Porter, *Competitive Strategy* (New York: Free Press, 1980). For an interesting elaboration of the product cycle model questioning the extent of the buildup in petrochemical facilities in hydrocarbon-rich countries, see R. M. Auty, "The Product Life-Cycle and the Location of the Global Petrochemical Industry after the Second Oil Shock," *Economic Geography,* October 1984, pp. 325–338.

For information on the innovative process and the location of innovative activity, see Sanjaya Lall, "Monopolistic Advantages and Foreign Involvement by U.S. Manufacturing Industry," *Oxford Economic Papers,* March 1980; D. B. Creamer, *Overseas Research and Development by United States Multinationals, 1966–1975* (New York: The Conference Board, 1976); Robert Ronstadt, *Research and Development Abroad by U.S. Multinationals* (New York: Praeger, 1977); R. Vernon, *Storm over the*

Multinationals (Cambridge, MA: Harvard University Press, 1977), pp. 43–45; and T. J. Allen, *Managing the Flow of Technology* (Cambridge, MA: MIT Press, 1978).

8. The following four paragraphs draw heavily from Vernon, "The Product Cycle Hypothesis in a New International Environment," pp. 255–267.

9. F. Schuller, "Foreign Innovation by U.S. Multinationals," DBA thesis, Harvard Business School, 1982.

10. For evidence of the slowdown in innovation, see chapter 9, above. Chapter 2 discusses minor and major innovations.

11. For discussions of competitive strategies, see Michael E. Porter, *Competitive Strategy: Techniques for Analyzing Industries and Competitors* (New York: Free Press, 1980); *Competitive Advantage: Creating and Sustaining Superior Performance* (New York: Free Press, 1985); "From Competitive Advantage to Corporate Strategy," *Harvard Business Review*, May–June 1987, pp. 43–59; and "Competition in Global Industries: A Conceptual Framework," in Michael E. Porter, ed., *Competition in Global Industries* (Boston: Harvard Business School Press, 1986), pp. 15–60.

12. The role of manufacturing specialists is discussed in chapter 4. For a discussion of Vista Chemical, see *The Economist*, May 16, 1987, p. 76.

13. For discussions of conditions existing in the first half of 1987, see *Chemical Business*, March 1987, pp. 12–15; *Chemical Marketing Reporter*, April 6, 1987, pp. 33, 36, 39, and 40; April 13, 1987, pp. 3 and 22–24; and May 11, 1987, pp. 3 and 57.

14. For a general discussion and description of the specialty chemicals industry, see United States International Tariff Commission, *Shift from U.S. Production . . . .* For other estimates of size, categories, and growth rates, see *The Economist*, October 29, 1983, p. 76, September 22, 1984, p. 90, and May 16, 1987, p. 77; *European Chemical News*, September 10, 1984, pp. 12–13; *Chemical & Engineering News*, June 4, 1984, pp. 20–23; *Chemical Insight*, Early March 1986, pp. 5–8; and *Chemical Business*, April 1987, pp. 10–13. For a focus on new materials, see the five "technical features" in *Chemical Engineering Progress*, June 1986, pp. 33–62. For a broad comparison of specialty and commodity businesses in the chemical industry, see John Forgrieve, "Role of Technology in Specialty Chemicals Business," *Chemical Engineering Progress*, August 1986, pp. 41–45.

15. *European Chemical News*, September 10, 1984, p. 12.

16. See note 14.

17. Profitabilities are taken from Compustat financial data base. For excellent discussions of the desire of management to escape the discipline of a product market by diversifying into other products, see Gordon Donaldson and Jay Lorsch, *Decision Making at the Top* (New York: Basic Books, 1983), and Gordon Donaldson, *Managing Corporate Wealth* (New York: Praeger, 1984).

18. Howard H. Stevenson and Jose Carlos Jarrillo-Mossi, "Preserving Entrepreneurship as Companies Grow," *The Journal of Business Strategy*, Summer 1986, pp. 10–23.
    For a case study, see David A. Garvin and Artemis March, "Allstate Chemical Company: The Commercialization of Dynamism," (Boston: HBS Case Services, Harvard Business School, 1986).

19. For a view that emphasizes the existing situation in petrochemicals versus specialties, see Peter Godfrey, "Specialty and Fine Chemicals, A Panacea for Profit?" Chem Systems Inc., November 1982, as reported in Joseph L. Bower, *When Markets Quake: The Management Challenge of Restructuring Industry* (Boston: Harvard Business School Press, 1986), p. 62.

20. *The Economist,* May 16, 1987, pp. 76–77.

21. Methanol is an obvious exception. See chapter 9, above, for a discussion of imports of methanol into the industrialized countries.

22. See chapter 6, above, for a discussion of technology sales and see chapter 9, above, for evidence that the hydrocarbon-rich countries will specialize in commodity petrochemicals for which technology is readily available for purchase.

23. See chapter 7, above, for a discussion of "balancing exports."

24. A basic description of these arguments is found in Paul A. Samuelson and William D. Nordhaus, *Economics* (New York: McGraw-Hill, 1985), pp. 865–866. I have focused on the industrialized countries, which obviously face different conditions than do the developing countries. As noted, the first argument for protection, "infant industry," applies to developing countries. But given the strong, long-term competitive positions of the hydrocarbon-rich countries, an argument can be made that the best policy for capital-short, hydrocarbon-poor developing countries is non-entry into the petrochemical industry. See M. A. Adelman and Martin B. Zimmerman, "Prices and Profits in Petrochemicals: An Appraisal of Investment by Less Developed Countries," *Journal of Industrial Economics,* June 1974, pp. 245–254.

25. *The Economist,* March 9, 1985, p. 18; *Financial Times World Petrochemical Analysis,* June 14, 1985, pp. 1–2 and June 28, 1985, pp. 1–3; and *Chemical Insight,* 327, Early October 1985, pp. 1–3.

26. The chemicals are benzenoids, which are a subgroup of synthetic organic chemicals (including a few that would classify as petrochemicals) granted special protection in 1922 in order to encourage the creation of a domestic industry so that the United States would not be dependent on German imports. As a result of the Tokyo Round of multilateral trade negotiations, the special protection ended January 1, 1987. (The American Selling Price method of tariff valuation, which was part of the special protection and under which tariffs were calculated by applying the ad valorem rate to the wholesale price in the United States instead of the export price in the country of origin, was terminated July 1, 1980. Following that, there were staged tariff reductions.) In 1984, the year for which the "over $1 million for each job saved" was estimated, the output of the domestic benzenoid industry was about $52 million (or substantially less than 0.1 percent of that of the overall chemical industry). See Gary Clyde Hufbauer, Diane T. Berliner, and Kimberly Ann Elliott, *Trade Protection in the United States: 31 Case Studies* (Washington, DC: Institute for International Economics, 1986), pp. 55–62. The estimates of the cost to consumers of one job for the 31 case studies, in a variety of industries, ranged from $30,000 to over $1 million; see pp. 14–15.

   The argument that it is more effective for a government to concentrate on monetary and fiscal policies rather than to single out an individual industry for protection appears in many places. A recent one is Robert Z. Lawrence and Robert E. Litan, "Why Protectionism Doesn't Pay," *Harvard Business Review,* May–June 1987, pp. 60–69. Similar arguments appear in Robert M. Stern, ed., *U.S. Trade Policies in a Changing World Economy* (Cambridge, MA: MIT Press, 1987), especially chapters 1, 3, 5, and 10; Paul R. Krugman, ed., *Strategic Trade Policy and the New International Eco-*

nomics (Cambridge, MA: MIT Press, 1986), especially chapter 9; and John C. Hilke and Philip B. Nelson, *International Competitiveness and the Trade Deficit* (Washington, DC: Federal Trade Commission Bureau of Economics Staff Report, May 1987). Also, see Gary Clyde Hufbauer and Jeffrey J. Schott, *Trading for Growth: The Next Round of Trade Negotiations* (Washington, DC: Institute for International Economics, 1985); and Gary Clyde Hufbauer and Howard F. Rosen, *Trade Policy for Troubled Industries* (Washington, DC: Institute for International Economics, 1986). For a more industry-specific view of the problem, see George C. Lodge and Bruce R. Scott, eds., *U.S. Competitiveness in the World Economy* (Boston: Harvard Business School Press, 1985). For an analysis of the adjustment of the U.S. petrochemical industry to the downturn of the early 1980s that indicates the "hands-off" policy of the United States worked better than the "hands-on" policies of Europe, see Joseph L. Bower, *When Markets Quake: The Management Challenge of Restructuring Industry* (Boston: Harvard Business School Press, 1986). For a study of a related issue, see Robert E. Lipsey and Irving B. Kravis, "The Competitiveness and Comparative Advantage of U.S. Multinationals, 1957–1983" (Cambridge, MA: National Bureau of Economic Research, 1986), Working Paper No. 2051.

27. This subject is of obvious concern to governments and companies. In the United States, for example, the Environmental Protection Agency estimated that in the five years ending in 1985, at least 6,928 accidents involving toxic chemicals occurred, killing more than 135 people and injuring nearly 1,500; see the *New York Times,* October 3, 1985, p. 1, D22. Although companies have always been concerned with the subject, my interviews with executives indicate that the Bhopal accident caused management to emphasize programs to prevent leaks of any kind. See also, *Business Week,* December 24, 1984, pp. 52–61, and *The Wall Street Journal,* Monday, November 11, 1985, pp. 1, 18.

   For a study of how five countries—the United States, Japan, Great Britain, France, and Germany—handled the problem of regulating vinyl chloride monomer, see Joseph L. Badaracco, Jr., *Loading the Dice: A Five-Country Study of Vinyl Chloride Regulation (Boston: Harvard Business School Press, 1985).*

28. For example, see *Chemical Marketing Reporter,* April 27, 1987, pp. 27, 28, and 37. For discussions of hazardous waste management in the United States, see *Chemical Engineering Progress,* July 1986, pp. 50–53, and Ronald M. Whitfield, "Superfund and the International Competitive Position of the Chemical Industry," presented to the Subcommittee on Commerce, Transportation and Tourism of the U.S. House of Representatives Committee on Energy and Commerce, March 21, 1985, Washington, DC.

29. International Convention for the Prevention of Pollution from Ships (known as MARPOL 73–78), by the International Maritime Organization.

30. See my chapters 4 and 7, above. Of course, any definitive conclusion about the new economic benefits of any action must consider all alternative uses of the resources, an exercise well beyond the scope of this book.

31. For a discussion of the slowness of the EEC to eliminate internal trade barriers, see *The Economist,* May 10, 1986, p. 48.

32. For a discussion of the United States and GATT, see John H. Jackson, "Multilateral and Bilateral Negotiating Approaches for the Conduct of U.S. Trade Policies," in Robert M. Stern, ed., *U.S. Trade Policies in a Changing World Economy* (Cambridge, MA: MIT Press, 1987), pp. 377–401. For discussions of the view in 1987 of the U.S. chemical industry on trade reform, see *Chemical Marketing Reporter,* April 13, 1987, pp. 3, 27; *Chemical & Engineering News,* April 27, 1987, pp. 7–13; and *Chemical Marketing Reporter,* May 11, 1987, pp. 3, 31. For a general discussion of the violation

by foreigners of U.S. trademarks, patents, and copyrights, see *Forbes,* November 17, 1986, pp. 40–41.

33. On patents, see Richard C. Levin, "A New Look at the Patent System," *American Economic Review,* May 1986, pp. 199–202. For evidence on the return from government direct subsidies, see Edwin Mansfield, "Public Policy Toward Industrial Innovation: An International Study of Direct Tax Incentives for Research and Development," in Kim B. Clark et al., eds., *The Uneasy Alliance: Managing the Productivity-Technology Dilemma* (Boston: Harvard Business School Press, 1985), pp. 383–407; and Edwin Mansfield, "The R&D Tax Credit and Other Technology Policy Issues," *American Economic Review,* May 1986, pp. 190–194. For the generic support argument, see Richard R. Nelson, "Public Policies of Support of Technical Advance: The Market Context, a Taxonomy, and an Appraisal of the Record," Yale University photocopied typescript, n.d.

34. A number of possibilities for U.S. government policy, including a number of those mentioned above, are discussed in U.S. Department of Commerce, *A Competitive Assessment of the U.S. Petrochemical Industry,* (Washington, DC: August 31, 1982), pp. 50–55.

INDEX